Andrew Clitherow is Directo
Blackburn and a Canon Resi
He is the author of *Into You*
Holiness in Everyday Minis
Renewing Faith in Ordained
Clergy (SPCK, 2004).

CREATIVE LOVE IN TOUGH TIMES

CREATIVE LOVE IN TOUGH TIMES

Andrew Clitherow

SPCK

First published in Great Britain in 2007

Society for Promoting Christian Knowledge
36 Causton Street
London SW1P 4ST

On p. 56, 'Cuttings' by Theodore Roethke, from *The Collected Poems of Theodore Roethke*, published by Faber and Faber Ltd, is printed with permission; on p. 92 an extract from *Hebridean Altars* by Alastair Maclean is reproduced by permission of Hodder and Stoughton Limited; on p. 104 lines from 'Aubade' from *Collected Poems* by Philip Larkin, published by Faber and Faber Ltd, are printed with permission.

Every effort has been made to acknowledge fully the sources of material reproduced in this book. The publisher apologizes for any omissions that may remain and, if notified, will ensure that full acknowledgements are made in a subsequent edition.

British Library Cataloguing-in-Publication Data
A catalogue record for this book is available from the British Library

ISBN 978–0–281–05885–3

1 3 5 7 9 10 8 6 4 2

Typeset by Graphicraft Ltd, Hong Kong
Printed in Great Britain by Bookmarque Ltd, Croydon, Surrey.

For my children,
Simon and Kate,
Emily and Edward,
who are a constant source
of joy and inspiration
to me.

It is good to believe in the God
who gives you the way
to believe in yourself
and in the eternity
of your becoming
to fall in love with the God
who is in love with you.

Dad

Contents

Acknowledgements

With very special thanks to my wife, Rebekah, for her patience, encouragement and love.

Thanks also to Dr Elizabeth Anderson for introducing me to the complexities of neuroscience and for her most helpful critical analysis of the text, to the Revd Dr Stephen Hunt for his advice and the Revd Dr Saskia Barnden for her extremely helpful comments and suggestions.

In addition, I would like to express my gratitude to Alison Barr at SPCK and Elizabeth Marsh for their support.

Introduction

Evolution is saving the group, not just the person, because it would seem that saving the group saves the person.[1]

Christianity, on the other hand, is saving the individual, not just the group, because it would seem that saving the individual saves the group.

Suffering: the black hole of faith for good people

We are living in a time when many people have had enough of religion. They've grown out of it. They abhor the perversions of many so-called religious people in many generations – not least our own – who manipulate faith for political ends and the abuse of personal power. They feel sorry for those caught up in unhelpful religious movements whose only desire is to discover an authentic faith that will make sense of their lives. But by all accounts, while many people have grown out of formal religion, they haven't had enough spirituality.

Growing up, however, can be a painful process. For in growing up we have to take increasing responsibility for ourselves. Society encourages us to be responsible adults while in the minds of many, the Church infantilizes us. As Western society becomes more self-aware than ever, the Church is seen as an institution that actively inhibits self-awareness and the processes that lead to personal maturity. As a friend of mine said recently, 'You cannot take what the Church offers as Christianity – there's something wrong with it.'

At a time when science and technology are almost daily providing us with new information about the nature of the life of the planet together with innovative means of design and communication, there are those who struggle to see any relevance in religious stories of a supernatural kind that come from a vastly different culture a very long time ago. Even from the earliest days in the history of the Church, there have always been those who have struggled with the ideas the Christian religion has sometimes attributed to Jesus. But there are few who would disagree with the overriding longing of Jesus that we should 'love our neighbours as ourselves'.

At a time when we are threatened by terrorism on a global scale, I suppose we can more readily grasp those aspects of the teaching of Jesus that are to do with promoting loving relationships. And if we could find the way for human beings to love their enemies as Jesus exhorts us to, we might feel a lot safer in a world where there is very significant religious and political unrest between nations of different faiths and ideologies. What is more, few would disagree with the teaching of Jesus about the need to work for social, political and economic justice.

But even if we cut out the supernatural religious elements from Christianity and concentrate on the personal and social, sooner or later we come up against the problem of pain and suffering that requires something more than social ethics to sort it out. While we might have a nodding acquaintance with God, an intuitive awareness that 'he's out there somewhere' and fundamentally on our side, when we encounter intense suffering we suddenly find the paint beginning to run on our picture of a God of love. Most of us at some time or other ask ourselves the question, 'Why did God make the world like this? Couldn't there have been a better way?' And that's when the growing up has to begin.

I have always found the problem of evil and suffering to be the greatest challenge to any kind of belief in a God of love who created the world, the universe, you and me. In common with many others, I find it to be the black hole of faith. And the godlessness of this darkness is all the more intimidating as it sits so uncomfortably and incongruously alongside our experience of a world of magnificent and intricate beauty. Our suffering – and the suffering of others – seems senseless most of the time in contrast with the happiness, joy, exhilaration and fulfilment we know well and frequently celebrate.

There seem to be three particular areas of evil and suffering that make a belief in a God of love pretty impossible. These are as follows.

First, we see not only beauty and blessing in creation but also evil and suffering. We like to think that God is a reality for us from what we know about the life of Jesus Christ and also from what we discern about the divine potential of every human life. Yet the natural world itself – supposedly the handiwork of a loving God – can perform its own crucifixion of the innocent almost effortlessly. Images of drowned and suffocated children in unexpected floods and mudslides in South America or as a result of freak weather conditions in central Europe don't inspire much confidence in a loving creator. Those who have loved and lost know that the greatest pain of all can come from a broken heart. God-forsakenness[2] is not confined to the crucified Christ. It is rather the sum of human suffering both before and since the death of Christ.

Second, some people seem to suffer to an unreasonably sickening degree when their pain is the result of human wrongdoing. Who can know what was really behind the infamous terrorist attack on the twin towers in Manhattan on 11 September 2001 and other subsequent atrocities? The blood of the mother and daughter huddled together as their hijacked plane crashed into the tallest office block in New York cries out against easy concepts of justice and theories of cause and effect. This kind of suffering can be caused by those whose understanding of themselves has itself been distorted or even destroyed by undeserved pain. But this pain cannot be understood as a proportionate effect of the lack of love in anyone's life. Neither is it a judgement on those who themselves have chosen evil ways. Nor can it be justified by the good that may arise out of it.

Third, there is the intractable problem of the apparently random way the innocent suffer through no fault of their own or anybody else. I remember hearing about a man whose fiancée had died from a rare disease. He fell in love and married and settled once again. He was fulfilled through the lives of their two children but before long lost his wife in a freak car accident. Here life seems to lack any sense.

This is but the briefest glimpse of the black hole of faith that causes many to abandon any kind of working relationship with God. It is appalling to think that a God of love could be responsible for having created a world that can be both so thoroughly good and so demonically evil. Like the black holes in the outer universe, this one has its own centrifugal force. Its enormous power threatens to annihilate any residual faith we might have in God and humanity. But we dare not get too close or ask too many questions. Sometimes we fear to rebel too much against our comfortable gospel of Jesus Christ and concepts of a loving creator God in case we are drawn into a place of darkness and faithlessness from which we do not have the resources to return. And then we shall be in hell. But, as recent scientific research suggests, it may well be that black holes are also places of immense creative energy. As we know, the most threatening places can also be those where we feel we are most alive. Can life, therefore, really arise out of apparent death?

A contemporary journey of faith

In this unpromising environment and along with many others, I struggle to find a way to forge a more honest and viable understanding of God. I need to find a way to pray that develops rather than diminishes my faith in God. To do this will be both difficult and dangerous. Will added spiritual maturity mean that I shall have to leave behind a search for humility and a sense of the holy which seems to have graced some of the more enlightened Christians so effectively in previous generations?

I sense that if I can find some answers, my faith in God is likely to be stronger, livelier and more resonant with my life in the twenty-first century. But some will say that trying to take greater responsibility for one's faith is, by definition, a pretty faithless approach to God. While I don't agree with them, I am aware that by daring to ask deep questions about Divine purposes in the world I might be in danger of describing a world where I make myself into some kind of god. So this is a risky business and not for the faint-hearted. I have tried it and feel I may have seen a little of what it is like on the other side of this black hole. But whatever progress I may have made has come not through any skill or courage of my own but only as the result of my willingness to be energized by the power that has lured me irresistibly onward.

What follows, then, is not intended to be the final answer to anything. Nor is it an attempt to persuade others to think as I do. It is simply a brief account of the way in which I have come to find some peace with the God of love amid the suffering of the world. In so doing I have had to question many of the absurdities of institutional Christianity.

By integrating two of the most popular approaches to the problem of evil and suffering, this story does, however, offer a way in which we can find Christ as the ground of our lives, in our pain and suffering as well as in our loves and joys, and therefore in the very heart of who we are today. So while anyone reading this may not agree with my reasoning and conclusions, they may find, within the story, words that help them in the further expression of their prayers for healing love and a re-location of the Spirit of Christ. And this may make them question much of what we cherish about the Church.

I have divided this exploration of faith and love into five sections. In the first, 'Crying out of love', I look more closely at how we might understand the nature of God in times of suffering and death, protesting against easy answers that others might give us.

The second chapter, 'God, guilt and love', begins with a discussion of the two principal ways in which Christians have traditionally approached the problem of evil and suffering. The first offers a more static and fixed view of our destiny, while the other is more dynamic and open to change. Neither on their own, however, meets our needs today. We have to see if there is a way to understand how God and the world have fallen out with each other.

In the third chapter, 'Falling out of love', I look at how we can understand the use of myth and mystery today and how we sometimes speak of seeing, hearing and even touching God. Love becomes both the energy and goal of our search where truth becomes apparent even and especially in the most unlikely of circumstances.

Chapter 4, 'Emerging love', traces how, in a world where life is often finely balanced between triumph and disaster, the presence and power of authentic love can be recognized as having emerged through the processes of evolution in the life of the planet and human relations.

And finally in Chapter 5, 'Love in person', we discover that, free of unhelpful institutional overtones concerning the significance of Jesus Christ, we are able to see ourselves in a different light. By developing a deeper understanding of our selves, we are able to rediscover the identity of the God who is both with and in us. As a result, we find that by self-offering love we can reverse the demands of evolutionary survival so that our relations with others are no longer based on an extremely high degree of self-interest set against their needs.

A different perspective on the Christian way of life: moving on from the Church as it is

Embarking on a journey of exploration such as this may well make the reader question much of what the Church is seen to stand for. Those who have locked-down vested interests in the institution may find these questions difficult, demanding and altogether too threatening to consider. I hope that others within the Church who are faithfully slogging on but sometimes wondering why they bother to do so will find encouragement here as these questions resonate with the ones they have been asking for some time. And I hope that others outside the Church will find that these questions liberate them to believe that what they had always suspected may well be true. I hope they will see that in Jesus Christ there is a truth and faith that – though largely hidden by institutional Christianity – is of ultimate worth for human beings who, while making the most of the ongoing benefits of science and technology, realize that materialism does not by itself offer ultimate satisfaction for the human spirit.

It has always been my belief that Jesus Christ offers us a new way of life rather than a new religion. No matter how noble the intentions behind them, religious structures can quickly become an end in themselves. When they do, the demands of radical love are replaced by institutional interests. This is the problem with much of the 'churchiness' we come across today. We've got the balance seriously wrong.

Restlessness with the ecclesiastical status quo, therefore, is a recurring theme. Those who believe in a largely vicarious kind of salvation through Jesus Christ and those who regard the institution of the Church as the only way to experience the sacraments of the world will find much to criticize here. On the other hand, those who are prepared to think beyond such parameters may feel both empowered and set free from much in the Church that reduces them to the status of dependent children.

So there is a need to look critically at the institution at the same time as we try to rediscover the Spirit of Jesus.

A faith that keeps its followers in an infantile relationship with a domineering Father-God will, of course, always attract those who find growing up altogether too challenging. But they learn only a little because they are unable to let go – or they have not had the opportunity to work through – issues from their own childhood and upbringing. It is very important for the development of Christian spirituality that we are constantly prepared to move on and allow faith to grow with each generation. This has never been more important than it is today as the Church faces a very uncertain future.

Following the death and resurrection of Jesus, his followers had to learn how to live without having him with them in the same way as before. Now the Church has to learn how to move on with a new understanding of Jesus. Jesus, 'meek and mild', saviour of the world in sacred scripture is 'dying the slow death of irrelevance'.[3]

What is more, a church that is perceived to offer institutional religion more than healing love to a world constantly on the brink of war has some very deep questions to ask about its nature and purpose. The Church is not to be confused with the kingdom of God. It is quite definitely not a perfect human community in complete communion with God nor, for the most part, does it pretend to be. Instead, the Church is the place where the Word is spoken that gives us permission to move from childhood to adulthood, from having faith in God to having faith in ourselves and from having faith in ourselves to having faith in God.

Those who followed Jesus moved on in their faith after his death and managed to learn a new way of being with Christ. In their prayers and service of others, they began to understand the meaning of the words, 'I am in my Father, and you in me, and I in you' (John 14.20). By taking on this responsibility for themselves, they took responsibility for God. And by taking responsibility for God, they revealed his glory to the world.

We do not have the option of standing still in our faith today, either. For sin is none other than a refusal to grow in our relationships and develop as we should. For many it is clear that if the institutional Church today refuses this challenge, it will die. And quite rightly so.

However, when those who come to the Christian faith for the first time, and those within the Church who are tired of unworkable theologies, allow the Spirit of God to guide their growth into self-awareness, they can rediscover the glory of the gospel *in the midst of* the life of the world.

> For as the earth brings forth its shoots,
> and as a garden causes what is sown in it to spring up,
> so the Lord God will cause righteousness and praise
> to spring up before all the nations.
>
> (Isa. 61.11)

Andrew Clitherow
Blackburn

1

Crying out of love

How does God answer our prayers for those who are dying?

When I have prayed with those who were dying, I have encountered three kinds of situation in particular which ask fundamental questions about the nature of God and how prayer might be seen to 'work' or not as the case may be. The way I have chosen to describe these three situations is by telling the stories of three different people.

Yet, while these stories come from my ministry as a parish priest, the questions they raise will be very familiar to others who are engaged in many different kinds of Christian ministry. Indeed all who have experienced faithful bewilderment following the death of a friend or a loved one may have at some time or other reacted in a similar way.

At times such as these, our prayers are tested the most. We combine what prayer life we have with the earnest supplication of grief for fear of being separated from others for ever. These prayers, together with what often seems to be a natural intuition, can help us to keep ourselves together when life around us is falling apart. But if these prayers have natural flaws they will be exposed in the months of readjustment that follow great loss. And as the flaws reveal fissures hitherto unrecognized, we are given the opportunity to grow or go under. Faithful endurance, however, brings a more developed understanding of the gospel of Jesus Christ and a deeper life of prayer.

To reach this point, though, means that we have to ask some difficult questions. So let us turn now to the three situations I mentioned above which I shall describe through the true stories of three people. (I have not used their real names in order to protect their privacy.)

I can remember how I once went to hospital to pray for an elderly parishioner who had only continued failing health to look forward to. Harry was tired and fed up. His bodily systems were shutting down. He had told me previously that he was ready to die. On arrival, I found that he was asleep. So I sat beside him and I silently prayed to God in a traditional manner asking that he should spare Harry from further suffering. After a while, as I left Harry's bedside, I was drawn to the bed of another – much younger – patient across the ward where there was quite a commotion going on. I asked if I might be of assistance and my offer was readily accepted.

Jean was middle-aged and her cancer was inoperable. She had suffered for months. There was no hope for the healing of her pain and distress, or even any sign of her final release from them. Understandably, she was struggling to cope. So, too, were the relatives standing by her bed. They told me their story, asking me to pray that she be allowed to die. As you can imagine, I felt that in this particular instance it was right to do so. So standing around the bed we held hands. I prayed out loud in my own words, asking God that Jean should have a merciful release from her pain. When I had finished saying this prayer, I did something very stupid. I said, 'She'll be all right now.' And then I left. The words had just come out. I could not believe my ears. I immediately realized how thoughtless and unprofessional I had been. I had learned long ago the golden rule in such situations, 'Do not raise the hopes of people who are already in a state of nervous agitation when you have no hard evidence on which to base your opinions. Never try and predict how God might want to answer your prayers.' At the time I comforted myself with the thought that in one sense I knew that yes, Jean would be all right. In prayer the problem had been handed over to God. But I had not offered some careful and sensitive explanation of this interpretation to her family around her bed. Nevertheless, while I had broken the rule, in a curious kind of way I felt that it had been somehow right to say these words. I felt that they had been 'given' to me. I had a sense of a spiritual agenda at work far greater than any guidelines for conduct that I might have read.

The next day I returned to the hospital to visit Harry. On approaching him I found the bed opposite empty. I asked the doctor what had happened to Jean. He told me that she had died unexpectedly in the night. I felt as if the prayer of the previous evening had been answered. Doubtless, the relatives – whom I never saw again – would have thought so too.

It was as if the timing of the prayer – together with the proximity of the relatives and the presence of a priest, perhaps – had somehow effected the early dispatch of angels to rescue Jean. (I do not say this lightly; this is but one of several such instances I have come across.)

Anyway, I turned back and continued to pray with Harry. But death for him was not going to be a merciful release for a long while yet. Yet, here, too, we had the synchronization of patient, relatives and priest together with the desire both to let go and commit to God. However, he was not spared until he and his wife had endured even more pain and that terrible grief that is part of the dying process. The different fate of these two people who shared a hospital ward left me confused. I know we cannot predict the way God answers prayer. But I sometimes wonder whether because the process appears so random, it is any good praying at all. It seems that God has made up his (or her) mind already.

Or should we suppose that, rather than some divine miraculous intervention taking place, in the timing of the prayer, the proximity of the relatives and the presence of a priest, Jean had simply been able to stop fighting, let go and move herself on? Might this have been a case of justice for one patient and not for another in the same hospital ward? Had Jean acquired sufficient merit points to see her off to heaven? Had Harry yet to make some amends or find peace with family and friends – some form of reconciliation – before he was to be allowed to die? Were there matters he had yet to put in order for which he was being given extra time? Was there a hidden purpose connected with his spiritual growth – or that of his wife – that affected the timing of his final demise? Or dare we countenance the notion that in the absence of God, his body was simply too slow to shut down completely and the doctors and nurses too good at keeping him going?

In all of this I find feelings of justice, fair play and equality to be elusive. Does God work from on high, deciding when people should stay and when they should go? Or does he allow us to determine our own destiny? The discrepancies in the way different people depart this life throw up all kinds of difficult questions. And what part did my prayers or the prayers of others play? Some say that to ask such a question is wrong. We are not meant to know cause and effect in this way. But my prayers are meaningless, surely, if the only reason I am saying them is to leave everything to chance, even if it is God's chance?

The third story is different again from the ones I have just related. In this situation, faced with the intense suffering of others, I did not pray that someone should be allowed to die. Instead, I prayed earnestly to God to spare someone from death. For, on this occasion, nobody felt that it was right that this woman who was in her early thirties should die. There was no getting away from the harsh reality that death in this case would be the desecration of a life. Caroline was nowhere near reaching what we often refer to as the end of our natural time. She was young, physically fit, married with two young children and had everything to live for. She had contracted a disease abroad where she had been living at the time. Even now – some years later – I can still hear her rattling cough as she mustered up the strength to move from one room to another in her mother's home. The obscenity of her illness as it viciously attacked her immune system was matched only by her unbelievable courage.

She was so brave. She had every reason to cry out in anger to the heartless God who visited on her this illness which laid hideous waste to the love and life she had found and enjoyed. Yet she showed no trace of self-pity or bitterness. Just an iron will to survive.

So, with her and her family I prayed once again. Not for death and an easy release, this time, but passionately and powerfully for life. Not life in the hereafter but life in this world where everything had been going so well.

No one felt that Caroline should die like this. Nor did anyone think it right that her family should suffer in this way. Why should she be denied the joy of watching her children grow up? Of feeling their arms around her? Of joining in their laughter and sharing their tears? And why deprive two young children of so much love and security? Surely, life is hard enough.

Some months later, I held Caroline's hand as she lay in an intensive care ward and I prayed again. I begged God to save her. It seemed such a wicked waste. Now as I looked at her, I could see the tanned skin of this beautiful woman hanging from her bones in a mocking statement of the life that had been wrung from her bit by aching bit over many months. Yet, although she fought with such courage for so long, the AIDS virus did away with her in the end. But this was not all. God, how I wish it were. For, not only had she contracted the HIV virus through a blood transfusion some years previously, it was discovered at the time of her funeral that it had been passed on at birth to her four-year-old son. A time bomb ticking away in his little body. I was left wondering how on earth – and in heaven – a so-called God of love could permit such indiscriminate suffering in a world of his making. And such stories are by no means rare. In many sub-Saharan African countries they are commonplace. Would even a small miracle in this instance have been such an unreasonable expectation? And if not for Caroline, at least for her son? Or is it naive to expect the God whose Son blessed little children, healed the sick and raised the dead to do the same today?

I suppose I could feel guilty about my anger and frustration. But I have to express my feelings in order to be true to myself as much as anything. (I never thought that I had to put my rationality into neutral because I have a Christian faith.) Maybe I simply didn't have sufficient faith. Perhaps I didn't trust God enough. Maybe I was being theologically naive to think that in the grand design of things, prayers such as these could have any tangible effect. Perhaps my faith had been caught unawares and I would have understood more if I had been more faithful earlier on in my life.

But must we resign ourselves to a 'gentle' transition into that 'good night' against which Dylan Thomas raged? Shouldn't we, too, be raging at the dying of the light?[1] Does such suffering sit happily within the will of God? Or is the suffering and death of Christ, God's scream of agony at the injustices and evil of this world?

To reply simply that this suffering was brought to its consummation in the resurrection of Christ is to be in danger of making light of the problem of pain and evil. For to celebrate the joy of Easter without plumbing the depths of the cross is to overlook why there was a need for the disciples to know that Jesus had risen from the dead. Prayers of resurrection thanksgiving are especially poignant because they are preceded by prayers that speak of our overriding sense of abandonment by God.

To pray only in times of so-called certainty is to describe the contours of a God that we ourselves have drawn. This effectively changes the prayer of Jesus in Gethsemane from 'Not my will but yours be done' to 'Not yours but mine be done' (Luke

22.42). So prayers of protest are perfectly legitimate in times of darkness and the apparent absence of God.

Perhaps we need to begin at the end with our confusion concerning prayers at the bedside of those who are soon to die. For if we are to understand how God and life fit together, we have to have an understanding of how the processes of dying and death fit within the love of God. We hope also, if only for our own relatives and friends, that our absence will one day give meaning and context to our presence.

There have always been within the Church those who say that while our lives can appear insignificant in the eyes of this world, their true meaning lies in what they refer to as eternity. By contrast, there are other Christians who argue that this life is all there is and that there is no life in heavenly bliss at all after death. Instead of taking our bearings from another world or heaven that exists in a different dimension, fulfilment is to be found in the discernment of some kind of ultimate significance concerning who we are and what we do now.

I struggle, though, to rationalize the deaths of Harry, Jean and Caroline – and countless others – simply in terms of our experience of earthly existence. There seems to be no reason behind these events; no recognizable system in which a God of love might be operating. It all feels too haphazard.

Is prayer useless?

There is, of course, another very important area where evil is seen to operate within the natural order of the world in an indiscriminate and largely disordered way. To the situations I have already mentioned we may add earthquakes, volcanoes, hurricanes, diseases and such things as fatal snake bites. I am aware that good may come from some natural disasters in terms of the renewal of the earth's resources, but they can also cause catastrophic damage to the lives of many because of the suffering they inflict on individuals. The Asian tsunami disaster on Boxing Day 2004 that claimed a quarter of a million lives is but one grim example of this.

In these circumstances, it would appear that prayer makes no difference at all. And this is one of the reasons why those outside the Church have great difficulty in understanding a Christian approach to prayer. In a utilitarian society, it is clearly evident and proved beyond contradiction that, according to the laws of this world, prayer does not work.

Prayer is not supposed to be a device by which in a dark room we can convince ourselves that we are not alone. And this has direct implications for the ways in which we pray. For in this life we are largely on our own and it is important that we recognize this from the beginning. Alone not only in terms of an apparent absence of direct guidance from God but also in terms of the support we might hope to receive from the Church.

This sounds rather harsh. I am not suggesting that we cannot be guided by God and that the Church doesn't care. But we should be very careful when we make statements concerning the ways in which God is guiding us. It is very easy to let our imaginations run away with us and to hear God speaking to us in our own words. For most of the time, God is not as direct as this. Nor is he directive in the way we sometimes suppose. The kind of prayer that asks for miracles of deliverance by Divine intervention can desensitize us and make us even more unaware of our surroundings.

And yet, good faith has helped humanity cope with the implications of self-awareness. As John Polkinghorne says, 'A world that was once just an expanding ball of energy has become aware of itself, so that, through us, the universe *knows* that it was once an expanding ball of energy.'[2] Denis Edwards also writes:

> What a theologian can suggest is that, whenever there was the first, perhaps child-like self-awareness, then this can

> be seen as the beginning of human experience of a world of grace. This grace, understood as God present in self-offering love, was already there . . . in the rise of bipedalism, already there in the first forms of life, and already there in the origin of the universe.[3]

But as neuroscience is revealing increasingly how our minds function, we should not be surprised that as we develop our understanding of self-awareness and appreciation of grace, this has a major effect on our developing understanding of the nature of Divine life.

So as the life of the Church develops, it is being forced to relinquish its understanding of itself as being in the business of telling people what to believe. This can be frightening for some. They think that Christians who do not accept traditional authority have lost their faith. But surely this 'lack of direction' can only be for the good. Most of us nowadays don't want to be told what to believe, anyway. With the support of others, we prefer to find out for ourselves.

So at this time of the telling of the Christian story, we have to separate Christianity from institutional interests. In the development of human society 'Godly tribes' win in the long term because leaders who believe that they are subject to an ultimate authority have usually become better leaders than those who do not. (Bad leaders – plunderers – may lead a few away for a while but not for long.) But we have now outgrown the evolutionary benefits of religion – to this I shall return in the final chapter – with its unnecessary semantics and synods. And herein lies a great opportunity.

As we shed the restrictions of religion, we discover that the teaching of Jesus was even more radical than we had thought. For he wasn't trying to make sense of religion but was rather exposing the nonsense religion makes of human becoming. For it is not in the restrictions of the law that people are fulfilled but in the freedom of authentic love that we find our alpha and omega, our past, present and future, Jesus Christ, the same yesterday, today and for ever (Heb. 13.8). And people quite rightly resist religious superstructures that are seen to suffocate such authentic spirituality. So corporate answers no longer convince. And in many ways our salvation has become privatized. It no longer belongs to bishops but to ourselves. My salvation is my issue. My responsibility. For we in the West are tired of religious wars and the blindness and bigotry of sanctimonious sainthood. The role of the Church is changing. It no longer delivers authoritative statements of faith that we have to believe without challenge or else face exclusion from the worshipping community. Instead, the Church should help us find our own way to grow in faith and self-awareness and spiritual stature. So although the Church continues to exist, it is not going to do our thinking for us. Our 'alone-ness', therefore, is not about being left behind or forgotten. On the contrary, it has everything to do with the growth and empowerment of the individual by which we find ourselves at the centre of the life of God through Jesus Christ.

Now, therefore, as we square up to the problem of evil and suffering, we will have to work our own way through. No one else can do it for us. If the truth is to set me free as Jesus said (John 8.32), I have to own it in the very depths of myself.

This, of course, is nothing new. The understanding of God I find as a result of purifying my heart has never been a commodity I can beg, borrow or steal from others. Nor is it something the Church can sell me, although at times it has tried to. While we need the support and guidance of a faith community for balanced spiritual growth – be it an informal Celtic community or Anglican parish – it is only within ourselves, in our living and dying with God and the world, that new insight grows. It does no harm to be reminded of the warning given by Thomas à Kempis:

> Be assured of this, that you must live a dying life. And the more completely a man dies to self, the more he begins to live to God. No man is fit to understand heavenly things, unless he is resigned to bear hardships for Christ's sake.[4]

But if in so dying and living I eventually become responsible for bearing my own share not only of the joys but also of the burdens of the world, it will be inevitable that I shall want to do this not in isolation from others but in community with them. For isolationism only decreases my humaneness.

If I am open to myself in this way, I become open to others. Therefore, my salvation is bound up with the salvation of others, in sympathy with rather than apart from the salvation of this world.

Religious thuggery revisited

While it can still be said that salvation comes through Jesus Christ, it would be wrong to see this simply in terms of what he sacrificed for me; something which costs me little, if anything.

Jesus shows the way of salvation. Yet because I have been created as a rational being with the potential to give and receive love, God has given me the responsibility of working out my own salvation. I reject this gift if I surrender my growing self-awareness to an overbearing religious organization. Nor can I make a half-hearted attempt by simply leaving it to Jesus Christ who, as a religious scapegoat,[5] died for my sins (1 Cor. 15.3).

Psychoanalytic theory today suggests that scapegoating takes place when unwanted thoughts and feelings are unconsciously projected onto others. There is still evidence of this in the Church as 'Christians often repress and project those shadowy aspects of their characters that do not conform to the will of God onto scapegoats, who are then blamed for having these characteristics' as in the attitude of some towards the ordination of women to the priesthood and episcopacy and the attitude of many towards gay men and lesbians.[6] Anyway, I can't help thinking that if humanity had had more faith in its encounter with God in Jesus Christ, there would have been no need for him to die as he did. So should I fail in my search for my salvation I will not now be able to blame anyone else. And it is because I take this responsibility seriously, and refuse to subcontract it to others within the Church, that I have to protest.

I refuse to give so-called 'easy' answers to the problem of suffering and evil. For I now realize that I have to grow in faith independently of God, as it were. This does not entail the severing of spiritual links. It is instead a breaking away from a divine paternalism that makes my praying a kind of sacrifice that is external to my own process of maturing in faith. This apparent detachment paradoxically involves a deepening of the spiritual life as prayer becomes increasingly grounded in the processes of my growing up.

So I want to have a word with this so-called loving God who made the world and who – according to the witness of the early Church – cares for us as individuals to such a degree, it is as if the hairs on our heads are numbered (Matt. 10.30). For I cannot accept that God made the world as it is and that this is how he meant it to be, any more than I can literally believe that God cares less for us when our hair begins to thin.

There is no shortage, however, of those who will try and smother this protest by dropping a ton of theology on you in order to silence your cries. Such people administer an intellectual mugging that can leave you afraid to speak your mind for fear of sounding stupid. They refuse to surrender their self-conscious certainty that what they teach us is infallible. Such power-obsessed clerics and lay people in Christianity (and other religions) have tried for too long to inflict their brand of religion on good folk who want only to make some sense of life for themselves and for their loved ones. Religious fundamentalists use their faith to re-enforce basic, natural instincts way beyond what is good for the individual; their feverish evangelism frequently leads to the denial of the convert's freedom. There are still those in ecclesiastical hierarchies who demand unreasoning conformity and try to riddle with guilt others who will not play their game. Their clever arguments, however, leave my heart untouched. They speak about theology in terms of logic and suffering as a necessary condition for life and growth. But I want to talk about the processes of love.

They say creation runs by an ordered set of laws which if altered would result in chaos. But what if these laws are indiscriminate in the suffering they cause for many individuals? Do we have to say that the progress of the overall scheme is what counts above everything? Do we agree that if several million people get sacrificed here and there, it doesn't really matter? Are our consciences cleared by the belief that these suffering people will be rewarded and their needs addressed at the end time? For this seems to run contrary to what I read in the New Testament about the sacred and special significance of life.

I am not arguing that I want to know everything that God is and might ever be. Instead, I want to discover how best to plumb the depths of the mystery of life in order to find a way through my pain. And I want to do this in such as way that does not reduce me to the passive status of a faithful lap-dog. It is time for my faith to mature. I've begun with milk but if I am to grow, at some stage I have to move on to solid food (1 Cor. 3.2). If peace is to be found, it will not come by the suppression of our feelings but by our confrontation of them. Then, even if at the end of the day we still do not understand, at least we will have discovered a way of coping that enables us to grow through this mess.

We cannot deny that humanity has been given or acquired through the evolutionary process – whichever way we look at it – intelligence and the powers of reason and reflective thought. This generation more than any other is learning – sometimes at an alarming rate – how the systems of life operate. So we may legitimately ask, 'Why did a loving God create a cancer gene that indiscriminately attacks human beings of all ages?' We ask not just because we are intelligent, rational and resourceful in our research into life but also because we care. And sometimes even, we love. More importantly, we dare to believe that we care and love in an analogous way to the way God cares and loves. So in the pursuit of love, we try and push back the boundaries of our understanding of God still further.

This is not a purely intellectual exercise. We use our minds, but we use our hearts as well. Logic and reason need somehow to be combined with the irrationality of love. The two have to go together. It is one of those 'both and' occasions rather than 'either or'. Mind and spirit have to work together if we are to confront our pain and suffering in a balanced manner.

As regards the suffering caused by humanity in its abuse of the planet and its inability to live at peace with itself, we might say the issues are clearer than they are when we are considering natural evil. But if we are not careful, we can end up blaming humanity for all the evil in the world. For when we overlook the presence of natural evil, our relationship with a loving creator God becomes much more intelligible. And we can blame all evil actions on evil people. Moreover, shifting the blame from God to humanity leaves us free to keep in with him, while separating others into friend or foe.

Here we can place God at a distance from the world and from awkward questions about his apparently flawed creation. If we are successful in this, we can receive that absolution which is granted to the partially sighted who – while focusing on the destructive behaviour of human beings – are unable to see the enormity of the problem of natural evil. But while this is tempting, it will not do.

For who is to say that much of the suffering caused by human beings is not the result – direct or indirect – of inherited genetic or psychological flaws? And is God not ultimately responsible for creating our genes and our brains as well? So there is no escape for God. No excuse. Either way – natural or moral – God has to accept ultimate responsibility for at least the potential for evil.

Righteous indignation

I sometimes feel that while God bears ultimate responsibility for the existence of evil in the first place, humanity has been given the responsibility for putting things right. Even standing up to evil, though, is not straightforward. The outcome is seldom guaranteed. And here it is rare for our motives and methods to be blameless.

An eyewitness account of the aftermath of the dropping of the nuclear bomb on Hiroshima just over sixty years ago on 6 August 1945, the Feast of the Transfiguration of Christ, gives two horrific pictures of the immediate aftermath:

> A mother driven half-mad while looking for her child, was calling his name. At last she found him. His head looked like a boiled octopus. His eyes were half-closed, and his mouth was white, pursed and swollen.[7]

> Many of those who perished were literally turned into cinders, for at the core of the fireball, half-a-mile across, the temperature was an unbelievable 50,000,000 degrees Fahrenheit. Even granite melts in a temperature as high as that. The primeval power of the sun had suddenly and terrifyingly descended upon the earth without the benevolent screen provided by distance and atmosphere.[8]

These examples illustrate painfully the mixed morality we often like to impose in warfare. In this instance, it is simply not good enough to justify inflicting appalling suffering upon a nation because in the view of others it had become irredeemably evil. Surely, we have to admit now that evil means were used to defeat an evil regime, leaving millions of innocent citizens to suffer. So I ask myself: is there any way in which I can make sense of this mother's appalling suffering and the ghastly incineration of so many people?

The supreme irony here is that the suffering in this context is caused by those who are meant to be standing up for the God of Jesus Christ in the fight against evil. What hope is there when, even as we do this, we invariably cause further suffering on a similar scale to the one we are trying to defeat? In recent conflicts we have been more ready to accept that the sword wielded in our own hand even against evil regimes abroad is itself tainted with at least some sense of failure; the 2003 invasion of Iraq being but one example.

So even when we stand up for what is right, there are no easy distinctions between good and evil, no Christ-like criteria that avoid negative fallout. But if God wants us to take responsibility for creation and to grow through our difficulties, why is the whole process of promoting life so fraught with death?

Or are we observing here a kind of cosmic law which we can cope with better when we see it in operation in the natural world but cannot comprehend when it applies to human beings within the context of a creation by a God who is deeply caring concerning the fate of individual lives?

After all, death and resurrection lie at the heart of the Christian faith:

> The theme of new life being enabled by death of earlier generations occurs in the biological world, enabling more complex life forms to arise from simpler ones, with the same set of chemical elements being circulated over and over again in the biosphere. Indeed, we are made of materials that are lent to us for the period of our lives, incorporating in our bodies atoms that have been utilized by many thousands of living beings before us, and that will be utilized again by many thousands more after our death.[9]

So should we expect indiscriminate deaths and disasters to continue until humanity has developed to some omega point where we will have grown out of such anarchic relations?

Maybe, after all, there is a purpose of love in all of this? A grand design that humanity might grow to learn how to love without conditions as Christ loved? If so, I wonder what part I have to play and what role God is performing.

In the book of Proverbs, people who are caught out by sudden calamity are criticized because they were not prepared. They are told that they had been given ample opportunity to learn to respect God and acquire knowledge of him which should have helped them. Instead they chose to ignore him. As a result, when disaster strikes they hear in their panic not the voice of wisdom but instead a mocking laugh (Prov. 1.23–33). A similar warning is given in the New Testament in the parable of the Two Housebuilders (Matt. 7.24–27).

The trouble is that it is extremely difficult to come up with a way of working things out beforehand that will withstand the ultimate test. When life is going well, we tend not to want to know about how life can go wrong. Most of us end up having to learn how to cope while at the same time trying to resolve some pretty fundamental issues. So because of our lack of prior investment, we end up with a religion of resignation as opposed to a faith for the future.

Death – which can invade our relationships at any time – is silently dreaded and never welcome. At its best, it can bring an end to the physical suffering of one person while bringing the most terrible grief to another. But we must not be overcome by it. For if we allow it, this mourning sickness can deprive us of life.

A young man, having lost his wife in an accident, wrote in his diary:

> I cannot forget the emptiness of grief: the feeling of having one's inner being carved out, leaving only an empty

> shell at the mercy of the wind. Instead of living, I have to be content with going through the motions. I participate in life yet I do not feel involved. I feel numb, suddenly realising that I do not laugh much any more, except to put on a show of normality for others. I wonder whether I will ever be able to feel my emotions again.

If we are to continue our search for truth in these extreme circumstances we have, therefore, to return to that place deep within ourselves where the pain is most acute. If God does love us, it is here that he will meet us and here that we have to learn to pray or rediscover what prayer is all about.

Learning to see in new ways

I do not have the faith of Job.[10] If the challenge issued to him had been made to me or to anyone I know, Satan would have won. Moreover, I reckon that in a society where the Divine name is used as a principal word in a liturgy of invective rather than invocation, most of us would curse God for much less!

However, reflecting on this I can begin to see that in order to enter into a meaningful dialogue with God while we protest – and legitimately so – anger that is useful for a while, in the long term only gets in the way. Without in any way diminishing the strength of our protest, we have to let go of anger and righteous indignation when we decide we want to grow through this. If we fail to do this, we make our pain our friend and comforter and leave no room for God to take his place in our lives. And no room for us to take our place in his life.

While we have every right to feel a whole range of emotions that are quite natural at times of great loss, accusing and blaming others, hurling insults and rhetorical questions, judging and condemning fellow Christians will only help us ease the pain for a while. For righteous indignation puts off the day when we take responsibility for dealing with our pain ourselves.

Criticizing God – almost for the sake of it – has to be but the prelude to the search for a resolution of our pain and discomfort. It should not be allowed to become an end in itself. Being honest about how we feel can cause us to turn against God when things go wrong. But we know at the back of our minds that if we let the sun go down on our anger we can find ourselves transfixed in a state of self-justification (Eph. 4.26). Refusing to give in, we deprive ourselves of the possibility of further spiritual development, opting instead to become rather sad and pathetic figures in our dejection and self-pity. We need, therefore, somehow to find the faith of Job who did not give up on God despite having everything taken away from him.

Maintaining our faith in God, particularly when we feel we have every reason not to do so, will largely depend upon how we maintain our prayerful union with him. We tend to pray according to our personality type, understanding of God and our fortunes in life at any given time. But it is sometimes helpful to pursue a different perspective and a kind of praying that helps us see ourselves and the world in a different way from before. There are different aspects to this kind of praying and it would be wrong to suppose that those who develop a contemplative awareness are not subject to all the usual forms of temptation in prayer that everyone else experiences.

Contemplative prayer is not purely the preserve of a praying elite. Even contemplatives have occasions of doubt and inner confusion. Those who experience a unity of being with God can be distracted and, instead of pure love, experience loss and spiritual isolation. While on this earth, few remain inextricably bound to the heart of God all the time. Those who learn how to engage in this kind of awareness, however, cease to understand the world of physical sensation as any kind of end in itself. Our experience of it cannot be separated from our spiritual journey. Instead, a deep sense of union with God is found where spirit and matter fuse in the apprehension of a deeper meaning within and beyond. An intuitive spiritual awareness is a natural result of the discovery of this peace at the centre of one's being. As regards this particular exploration of suffering, contemplation comes as the result of a process of perception. Here I find I am able to see beyond the physical to the greater spiritual reality within. So it is not simply about looking at life differently but about being able to see further than before.

This spiritual perception comes as a gift when we move from activity to stillness. This does not mean that we cannot lead busy and active lives but that such lives are founded on a deep spiritual peace at the centre of one's being. This peace opens our eyes to the divine significance within all our relationships. As protest gives way to the pursuit of a unity of being, love opens the eyes of the beloved to the Divine Reality as the ground of all being. It also opens the heart to an unspoken dialogue between the Creative Spirit of the universe – the Holy Spirit – and the spirit of the individual.

Once begun, the exchange of Word and Wisdom flows continuously although we are not always aware of it. We are often ignorant of our subsequent union with the Divine because our concentration is diverted elsewhere. Yet when we make time to be still, the inner voice of creation and re-creation can again be heard. How much we listen is up to us. When 'on line' we are almost effortlessly swept along by the energies of divine love in creation. Here we are taken ever further away from the priorities of the physical to the inner stillness of the interrelatedness of heaven and earth.

However, while contemplation is in essence a natural activity – it should come naturally to all of us – this immediacy was lost in the Fall. ('Fall' here refers to the way humanity has 'fallen away' from the purpose God had intended for it or 'fallen out of love' with God. The traditional understanding of this is given in the Bible in the mythological story of Adam and Eve in Genesis 3.) Since that time the art of contemplation has been received as a gift and enjoyed by many as a way of returning to a close relationship with God. It cannot be earned as it cannot be learned, yet by the grace of God we can suddenly discover that we are in possession of it. As the unknown author of *The Cloud of Unknowing* writes:

> If you were truly humble you would feel the same about the contemplative life as I do, that God gives it freely, irrespective of merits. God's gift of contemplation is such that when it is present the soul can both practise it and know it is doing so. It is impossible to come by otherwise.[11]

The principal way to union with the Divine Reality and Truth is not, therefore, through anger. For anger cancels out love. Nor is it by knowledge. For God is in essence essentially unknowable. It is, rather, through a mystical union energized by love. To quote the author of *The Cloud* again:

> All rational beings, angels and men, possess two faculties, the power of knowing and the power of loving. To the first, to the intellect, God who made them is forever unknowable, but to the second, to love, he is completely knowable, and that by every separate individual.[12]

This is not a way to escape the harsh reality of life on this planet. This is no sentimental or emotional kind of love. It is unaffected by mood or whim. It operates at the level of spirit, being the motivation of the inner life:

> For love that is pure and perfect, though it admits that the body is sustained and consoled when such sweet feelings or tears are present, does not complain when they are missing, but is really pleased not to have them, if it is the will of God.[13]

The most moving moments of this mystical union are not experienced in some ecstatic ejaculation. Instead, they are to be found in a deep peace. This is a peace that lies beyond the self-help schemes of various current cosmetic short-term therapies and even the natural aphrodisiacs of the ancient past.

These moments come from a person's increasing desire and ability to participate in the continuous presence of the Divine Spirit of creation. By living in harmony with this Spirit that operates at the very deepest levels of life, persons develop a greater awareness of themselves and their surroundings.

As a result I become more present to the world around me. And even the most painful absence of God will not overcome this silent prayerful exchange unless, of course, I decide to walk away.

In John's account of the time when Jesus was preparing the disciples for his being taken from them, Jesus says:

> I have said these things to you while I am still with you. But the Advocate, the Holy Spirit, whom the Father will send in my name, will teach you everything, and remind you of all I have said to you. Peace I leave with you; my peace I give to you. I do not give to you as the world gives. (John 14.25–27a)

As I say, this prayer does not offer a way of escape but rather a deeper engagement with the world. Even here, however, the purposes of love are constantly challenged and threatened with extinction.

So if Truth is found by a dialogue between human and Divine spirits, it has to be a conversation of direct – rather than reported – speech. Moreover, it has to engage with the world itself as the place where God already is. Being a Christian is not about discovering a holy place that is somehow separate from the world. It is about entering into the holy place of the world in a new way.

This contemplation – that can be carried out both while one is still and on the move – can itself lead to fear. This is not a fear of personal extinction but a terrible concern that truth and love must triumph when on occasions the wickedness of humanity's self-interest can feel overwhelming. This prayerful journey will be hard for those whose eyes have come subconsciously to see the limits of reality in technology and scientific development alone. For just as contemplation cannot be earned, neither can it be gained second-hand. We have to see for ourselves. We have to recognize this prayer as a relationship based on an interaction between the spirit of the individual and the Spirit of creation. This will not be apart from but in and with our rapidly developing scientific understanding of reality. Science and technology – while frequently presenting humanity with the most searching questions as to the use and abuse of new knowledge – have greatly enhanced humanity's knowledge and way of life. They have brought relief from suffering in a way religious belief cannot, and sometimes despite it. And they will no doubt continue to do so for generations to come.

The danger – as far as the contemplative is concerned – is not so much the television or personal computer, in themselves. It is rather the temptation to allow the work of our hands to become the mirrors of our spirits. For when we permit this to happen, the image that we see of ourselves will be back to front, as we confuse the 'maker' (ourselves) with the 'Creator' (God). There is no doubt that science and technology offer windows into the creation of the universe as they unravel the make-up of created existence. But as they ease humanity's passage through this life, contemplative prayer can help us to see the Truth in all of this.

Most of all, if we are to experience the Divine Reality that can help us both with our joys and also with our pain, there is a need not only to look at but also to accept ourselves in order to find the ground of Being within. The journey deeper into myself – and therefore deeper into God – is about the right love of my 'self', together with an understanding of my origins and the dynamics of my personal development. This is the route whereby I can clear a space for my spirit and the Divine *Ruach*[14] to meet and co-operate.

The Church, however, is often misunderstood to be about constraining rather than celebrating this creativity. It is heard speaking of discipleship as a long, arduous and pretty predictable progression from repentance to salvation. Predictable in the sense that while you may feel an overwhelming need to conform to this plan, you know in your heart that you will never achieve its goal. For somewhere along this line, you will either condemn yourself or some self-important zealot will say or do something to condemn you.

Few lives, if any, progress easily within this linear scheme of salvation. And the Church has known this from the beginning. For its prayers reflect the need to repent daily because most of us tend not to live lives of linear progression but ones where we tend continually to revisit the same old places, neuroses, fears and temptations time after time. Our lives are more spiral-like than linear, but while we may be revisiting old haunts regularly, we hope to diminish the time we need to stay there. So we understand salvation better if we see it as a way to use our self-awareness for life rather than as a preparation for death. For as we become increasingly whole in ourselves, we can better relate to others for good, while at the same time diminishing our own agenda for self-satisfaction. So the contemplative self that surrenders to this process is not diminished but rather becomes greater than before, in being more whole and in touch with itself and the pervasive spirit of the universe.

This also means that there will be a subtle change in the way we pray on behalf of others. Without a contemplative awareness such as I have described, these prayers could well be offered as words that are almost external to the ceaseless Word of creation that binds all things together. Externalized to this degree, they fall into the category of sacrificial offerings to a remote God. Then we abuse the Spirit by trying to make our pleas more effective. Then when we don't get what we want, we become frustrated and angry.

By contrast, when we pray for those in extreme circumstances from within the life of the Spirit, we are at once in harmony with the creative processes of life. Our understanding of the nature of God alters as we begin to understand Jesus Christ as someone who is not unlike ourselves. Praying for some to live and others to die is replaced by an understanding of life that goes beyond a definition of 'success' and 'failure' in terms of life and death.

An appeal to mystery should not, therefore, inhibit the development of an informed faith for 'a perfectly good definition of Christian theology is "taking rational trouble over a mystery" . . . The question is whether we choose to wrestle with it, or take the lazy and complacent view that this is conveniently off-limits.'[15]

So while we haven't begun to find any 'answers' to the problem of evil and suffering, at least we now have a means to take us further towards where we want to be, for

> we need a good story, a moral landscape of admonition and promise for people who have sustained a bad Fall, but nevertheless seek a better city; and en route that story should tell them who is their neighbour, how to find a way home after prodigal expenditure in a waste land, and how to recognise a pearl of great price when they see it.[16]

So in this quest we seek to discover not only why others suffer and die as they do, but also why any of us should suffer and die. In searching for the truth of the Divine Reality – in the most uncomfortable areas for anyone to try and have faith in a loving creator God – we seek an understanding of eternal life in its original meaning in the Gospels. This is not simply the life we are meant to lead in the nearer presence of God following physical death. More importantly, it is the quality of Spirit-filled life we lead in the here and now and which we shall enjoy in all its fullness later on. Therefore, in seeking answers for others, we seek them for ourselves. In dealing with the darkness that surrounds others, we ask for light for ourselves. In facing the death of others, we plead that we might live.

This is, of course, only the beginning. We need to look more closely at the nature of prayer and our relationship with God before we can grow up a little more. We need to be able to see in more detail why some of the more traditional answers are no longer convincing.

2

God, guilt and love

Prayer, love and salvation

I am discovering what it means to be 'me' in my own right. Hitherto, I have tended towards a form of ecclesiastical prayer that has often externalized God from his creation. As a result my attempts to understand my identity and search for faith have been held back by a misunderstanding of the nature of God. To turn away from anger and a theology of protest and develop our understanding of prayer is to begin to take responsibility for life again. When we stop seeing ourselves as victims, or when we cease to project our victim status on to others, we begin to engage in the process of healing. And as we continue to ask searching questions about God, we find that increasingly we are asking questions that lead us to inquire more deeply about our own identities. Consequently, our life is re-orientated not by the majesty of creation or the magnificence of scientific knowledge, but around a form of prayer that involves us even more in the life of the world.

Whereas faith has largely – though not exclusively – been about the way we discover and relate to God, it seems to me that the rediscovery of the 'self' instead is the prime aim of our desire for spiritual development. Rather than praying to a God who is likely to crush my individuality, I find that the way to know Christ is by looking deeper within myself. Christian religion can become pretty meaningless when divorced from personal development of this kind. Moreover, the Church cannot be a healing community if it is not itself comprised of a community of people who have been healed and are themselves fully engaged in promoting the healing of the soul or spirit.

Traditional practice has to be understood and reinterpreted within the light of our current appreciation of the love of God. If we are not prepared to do this, the good news that is supposed to set us free is more likely to tie us down to historical beliefs and an ecclesiastical vernacular that eventually few can understand or own.

We have to face up to the awkward truth that images which worked in previous times may not work today. What promoted new life for one generation may result in the spiritual death of another. So while retaining our faith in Jesus Christ and the Church, we should not shy away from reinterpreting their significance for today.

Against this background, Christian contemplative prayer can cross boundaries of time and tradition. It has its roots in the earliest praying of individuals and communities. The Church – presently preoccupied by structural reorganization – needs ministers both lay and ordained who offer lives of contemplative prayer much more than it needs effective leadership and slick management.

What has changed is the way and the place from which we ask our questions and seek deeper union with God and ourselves. Instead of asking some omnipotent power why he allows this person to live and that person to die, I now ask to see further how the creative processes of life – in which I am now involved – came to operate like this in the first place. I ask not as someone who has no rights but rather as someone who is caught up within the prayer of the universe. And while I am full of wonder at creation, I see and feel its wounds as well. As I say, this prayer is not new. It is evident in the great traditions of mystical prayer and Christian theology. Our generation has forgotten it and we need to replace or reposition it within the world and the Church today.

It is no longer a case of trying to get a monarchical God to see things my way so that I might persuade him to change his mind. Instead, my praying cannot now be separated from my desire to see the triumph of the processes of creative love. I begin to realize that despite the vast size of the universe, the Creator is not distant after all. I am discovering him now as the basis of all life. And these wounds that I carry in common with many others are not just mine and theirs but his as well. So rather than sitting in church, I seek further meaning by plunging myself into this stream of life in which I am borne along. Once again I am fearful because, paradoxically, as I discover a new freedom in my relationship with Christ, I can at the same time feel as if I am losing control. The current of these living waters (John 7.38) is so strong I fear I may go under.

A growing understanding of unity between myself and the Spirit of creation – together with a deepening of the divine dialogue I mentioned before – has set me at odds with much of what I thought the Church was telling me about the nature of Christian belief. So at this stage, I experience both freedom and fear.

I feel as if I have been caught between two cultures of faith. The Christ I see emerging over the horizon looks radically different from the Christ of my traditional expectations. As the gospel stories are freed from the interpretation of corporate sentimentality, I might echo the words of John the Baptist, 'Are you the one who is to come, or are we to wait for another?' (Matt. 11.3). Like John, I find that a completely traditional understanding of God makes it difficult to recognize Jesus today.

The pressure of the old religion that has held me down with the weight of ecclesiastical convention did at least provide me with a sense of security. But at the same time it imprisoned me by manipulating my conscience through the unscrupulous use of negative guilt. The Church's unreasonable demands and expectations not only exposed a misunderstanding of the gospel but of human nature as well.

To approach human development with a list of 'thou shalt nots' we now know keeps individuals in infantile subservience to their natural innermost 'drives'. The result is a neurotic fear of human nature – particularly its darker side – and a fear of God that has led those enlightened by a deeper awareness of the make-up of the self to turn their backs on Christianity and the Church. But now as I grow up and release myself from the grip of overbearing religion, I find I have the power to give myself quite a fright. A sudden recognition of my own shadow can be terrifying. And sometimes I think it would be easier simply to be terrified of God. From time to time, in pursuit of spiritual regeneration, feelings repressed for more years than I care to imagine suddenly appear out of the darkness. Worse still, they hit me with a ferocity that leaves me at their mercy. Now, however, shame does not need to be the dominant emotion. I no longer need to conceal my feelings from a God who measures my worth against his perfection and from a church that appears to make respectability its overriding aim. Now I can be honest about my feelings, and in my growing understanding of them, as I learn to deal with them constructively.

I had been told that God allows us – or willingly causes us – to experience pain and suffering in order to draw us closer to him. He uses the fact that our prayers are most fervent when our pain is most intense. But I can no longer believe that God causes us to suffer calamity in order to make us pray more effectively. If the purpose of the spiritual life is loving union with God, then surely it does not make sense to say that God coerces our love in its most intimate expression, that is, when we are at prayer?

If the basis of prayer is a dialogue of love between the Creator and his creation, it can only proceed by love. I am not suggesting, however, that we are never led into times of suffering so that we might discover the power of redeeming love in them. Nor am I saying that love doesn't mean sometimes – usually at a critical moment in life – that God leaves me for a while in my discomfort for my own good. If God is constantly bringing me to my knees by sending misfortune upon me, I suppose I could understand this to be the action of a loving father who knows best for his offspring. But if my response to God is always conditioned by pain in this particular way, I will have little room to love God for himself.

The intensity of love that I seek should surely come as a result of my contemplation of Absolute beauty and love both in the magnificence and mess of creation rather than from a series of contrived calls for help. Prayers of adoration and thanksgiving provide the context for our prayers of supplication. And we have already seen how intercession becomes meaningless when it takes place outside the economy of the love of God.

So, above all, I want to love God for who he is. I don't want to be dependent upon him because he is the one who always rescues me when I am in trouble. I don't want to feel that I am constantly in his debt. Why can't I be trusted to rescue myself?

If the nature of God's love for me is only – or even predominantly – in terms of his being my saviour I have to assume that he has not after all created me as a cherished entity in myself. I cease to have unique and valued individuality. I exist only on the basis of his need. In parish ministry it is easy to fall into the trap of trying to become everyone's rescuer. Before you know it, your care for others has become centred around your need to be rescued from your own lack of identity. Rescuing or saving ministry sits less well with incarnate love, with that empathetic, identifying, co-suffering companionship we find in Jesus Christ. If God's prime function is to save me, I can only conclude that his love for me is flawed; that there is a lack of balance in the heart of God. He wants to use me rather than love me. While I feel it is right to turn to God when I am in need – humanity cannot achieve all it is called to do without being grounded in God – he is there neither as my saviour nor as my judge. While God in Christ brings the *possibility* of salvation and judgement to the world and to myself, I do not find I can achieve new life by simply accepting the doctrine of others. Nor do I feel I am likely to develop as a person if I appropriate the life of Christ to fill the wastelands of my intellectual doubts.

The idea of this divine manipulation of love is absurd if we believe that the nature of the Creator God – as the source of all authentic love of the universe – is without blemish. I find it more helpful to speak of God in terms of his being the perfect source of all true love while I recognize that this love is to some extent incomplete in creation.

So God does not force me – or anyone for that matter – into a praying union of love. Nor does he keep me there against my will. Instead, it is because authentic love remains unfulfilled in creation that we look to him for help on a day-to-day basis and particularly when we feel we need it the most.

While we have turned away from anger and protest, there is no condemnation in an honest search for the truth. There is no need to think that continued questioning indicates a regression into protest. For this 'Way' love is taking the place of the anger I once felt.

So to be reborn means that, thanks to God, I learn how to be myself in a different way from before. I do this by learning how to become 'another Christ' as a result of my locating the ground of love within my life. Gerard Manley Hopkins says, 'What I do is me: for that I came.'[1] In being me I ground my life in God. In co-operation with God I either achieve my own salvation or bring about my own judgement:

> Indeed, God did not send the Son into the world to condemn the world, but in order that the world might be saved through him . . . And this is the judgement, that the light has come into the world, and people loved darkness rather than light because their deeds were evil. For all who do evil hate the light and do not come to the light, so that their deeds may not be exposed. But those who do what

> is true come to the light, so that it may be clearly seen that their deeds have been done in God. (John 3.17, 19–21)

So it is the location of love in my life – together with my desire to see it flourish in the world – that makes me active in the pursuit of my own salvation.

What drives me to prayer is not fear, but rather the purposes of love that I have already detected in the universe. Being thus committed to the dialogue of God's love, I am therefore critical of those prayers that leave me imprisoned and unable to understand how my faith can have any real impact on the progress of love.

If this exploration of suffering is to have any meaning beyond spiritual self-indulgence, the prayer it produces has to be one that celebrates and promotes the healing love of Christ in the world. So the more I can allow Christ to help me save myself, the more I can offer his saving love to others.

In this sense, self-knowledge leads to salvation. This is as true today as it was for Thomas à Kempis in the fifteenth century:

> All perfection in this life is accompanied by a measure of imperfection, and all our knowledge contains an element of obscurity. A humble knowledge of oneself is a surer road to God than a deep searching of the sciences . . . At the Day of Judgement, we shall not be asked what we have read, but what we have done.[2]

Distortion of love and a misunderstanding of myself

This approach in turn poses more questions. And more insecurity. Having moved on to such a degree, I find I am in danger of leaving others behind. I no longer think or believe as they do. Does this make me a heretic? Have I prayed myself out of the Church?

While desperately longing for a re-formation of the Church today which re-establishes Christ at the centre of the life of society, I have serious questions concerning how others within the Church continue to rationalize the problem of pain and suffering. While I have already alluded to these views in my own experience, I want now to consider them in some more detail as they are expressed by others.

I remember a conversation I once had with one of the mourners following a funeral I had just conducted. Speaking with her made me realize how the victim culture had become institutionalized. (While the following is the view of a decreasing minority, returns to a fundamentalist faith regularly produce a resurgence in this way of thinking at either end of the ecclesiastical spectrum. While not as prevalent as it once was in this country, this approach is central in some other countries.)

I was walking away from the graveside and expressing my sympathy to Judith, the sister of the deceased who had died prematurely at the age of 46. Judith simply replied, 'Ah, well, it is God's will.'

Judith – a secondary school teacher – was a regular churchgoer and committed to the Christian faith. She spoke further about what she meant by this extraordinary statement at the 'do' afterwards in the local pub. Since then she has been happy to discuss the matter with me on several occasions. While there had been plenty of meaning in the life of her sister, there seemed to be no meaning behind her death.

Judith had come to the conclusion that an omnipotent God has at some time decided what will or will not happen to us and that, powerless to alter this situation, we should leave it at that. God decides when we live and die. Leaving it to him is what having a faith in God is all about. It's about trusting that whatever happens is right. Drive on the wrong side of the road if you must, you'll only die when it is your time according to God's schedule.

I came across this again more recently when at 20,000 feet the pilot of the passenger jet I was in struggled to maintain control of the aircraft for some twenty minutes. A fellow passenger sitting behind me was trying to comfort a woman who was very distressed. 'Don't worry,' he said, 'I've always believed that if it's your time to die, then your time is up and there's nothing you can do about it.'

This wasn't exactly what she wanted or needed to hear. This situation had been caused by a mechanical fault. No more and no less. We had taken a calculated risk getting on to the plane in the first place. This wasn't anything to do with God and his predetermined plan for those on the aircraft. It was about the fragile nature of life on to which we superimpose semi-permanent qualities.

To adopt Judith's position is to take a backward step in our search for meaning if only because it belongs to that understanding of God that locates him primarily in terms of being 'out there and over us'. God stands with Peter his superintendent ticking off the names on his clipboard as the hapless souls – some with steady gaze, others surprised – stagger their way through the heavenly portals.

To entertain Judith's concept of God is to understand him as an authoritarian figure, detached from this world and largely unaffected by it. She seems to be saying that having made the world out of nothing, he has the right and power to do what he likes with it. This God is like a remote and powerful head of state. He will do whatever is required for the good of everyone while paying scant regard to the needs of the individual. If some die earlier than others in order to preserve the well-being of heaven then this is how it has to be. Moreover, when someone dies, be they three or a hundred and three years of age, this is the result of a decision of the omnipotent God who sees everything and makes all decisions of ultimate worth. Whenever we die, therefore, it is the right time because it is God's time.

But more than this, Judith holds that the way we live has also been predetermined to a large extent by God. She believes that before God made the world there was a falling out in heaven.

Some angels had been created more complete than others. Those who were less than full of the divine love decided that they would live apart from God. The result is that since the creation of the world, this falling out has infected humanity. We have inherited the guilt and condemnation of those first angelic beings. The sin of Adam is at the same time the sin of all his descendants who are seminally linked to him.

So there is no independent force of evil that causes life to go wrong and brings about the many deaths that plague us. While creation is wholly good, in those people where goodness is absent – to a lesser or greater degree – there has been a significant turning away from God. Evil exists therefore only as a perversion of something that was originally good.

Judith finds consolation in the belief that while we make a mess of our lives as a result of our own free choices, God saw long ago that we would do this and provided the means by which some would be saved and others would not.

God repairs the effects of sin by intervening in human affairs and distributing proportionate punishment. Judith says we begin life as sinners – infected by the original sin of Adam and Eve – and live in a state of constant guilt and condemnation. Somehow through our faith we have to use our free will and – making enough of the right decisions – get back on good terms with God. By using the sacrifice of Christ to effect our acquittal, we ensure that our final destination will be heaven rather than hell.[3]

It is clear that in terms of finding a way of coping with suffering today, Judith's model still provides some peace of mind for many. I think it only works because it allows us to file the difficult underlying questions in such a way that it becomes possible to carry on living while being surrounded by an absence of answers.

For Judith, God is the sole arbiter of truth. We have to make sure that we keep on the right side of him, hoping that our friends and relatives do the same. We pray with the psalmist, 'If you are silent to my prayers for help and justice, I shall be like the workers of evil who go down to the Pit, being subject to divine punishment' (Ps. 28).

I have to say that I find this response to suffering and evil abhorrent. How can love be central to my prayers when I am dealing with a God who bears many of the traits of a despotic dictator?

Nothing of what I do, or do not do, seems to affect this deity. He is out of reach and out of touch. What is more, my freedom to think and react to all kinds of moral and ethical questions becomes severely diminished. My individuality – which we have established as being central to the development of our faith – is to all intents and purposes ignored. I certainly don't feel cherished. And I am able only to investigate the created world within the strict confines of a divine moral code. Worst of all, the relationship I am meant to have with God is based not on love but on fear. How can it be my fault that aeons ago my angelic ancestors fell out with God? I don't mind – might even understand – them having a row with God, but why does it seem that I am bearing an unfair proportion of the blame? And what kind of life is it if one is constantly trying to keep on the right side of a God who might easily condemn you to eternal damnation anyway?

I think that Judith's understanding of the place of suffering within God's plans for creation produces a fake form of holiness. The outlook that she endorses permits her to divide others into those who are good and those who are evil. Those who are 'in' and those who are 'out'. Those whom God is going to save and those who are beyond the pale. If you go to church and say your prayers, you will go to heaven. If you don't, you will go to hell. So instead of working on the darker side of our nature, we have to hide it. Otherwise, we cannot remain within the community of vested interests. When anyone displays signs of social, political or religious nonconformity, they are dismissed and discredited in authoritarian statements disguised as God's righteous judgement. Those who are content to live by such repression and denial – enforced by strict religious codes which no one can in fact keep – are often led by an elite group whose holiness is due less to their purity of spirit and more to the good fortune of not yet having been found out.

In the event of discovery, the leaders themselves quickly become outsiders. They are understood to have 'given in to sin' and are guilty of contravening what is erroneously thought to be respectable behaviour. The judges are judged. And those who now do the judging happily ignore the principle of forgiveness behind Jesus' treatment of the woman caught in adultery (John 8.1–11). When human beings go astray, the Church responds, not according to the priorities of God's kingdom, but rather as if it were a primitive tribe whose sole purpose is survival by the purity of its membership. Thus all the usual biological patterns of behaviour that normally govern the survival of a tribe or primitive society can be reinforced by the Church. Yet I always thought the Church was supposed to embody a community that is free from instinctual behaviour.

Moreover, this God who claims to have endowed us with free will actually permits very little freedom in decision-making. When we make the wrong decisions – as we inevitably do – we are punished. So we experience good and bad fortune in this life in proportion to the amount of goodness or absence-of-goodness in our life. The gay man in the last stages of an AIDS-related illness is understood to be suffering as a result of the judgement of God. Verses are found in the writings of both Old and New Testaments and amalgamated in such a way as to pronounce a guilty verdict to which there is no answer, because those who abuse scripture in this way claim that they speak with the authority of God.

One of the most moving funerals I have taken was for a man who had died from AIDS. He had at various times been a pilot in the Royal Air Force, a civil servant and a teacher overseas.

He felt restless for much of his life as he tried to come to terms with his sexuality. Having worked through a disastrous marriage in which he had clearly tried to be someone other than he was, he eventually found peace and love in the arms of another man. Tragically, it cost him his life before he had reached the age of fifty. He died having contracted the HIV virus which developed into full-blown AIDS.

The love, however, that was evident at his funeral and the support, understanding and prayers on that occasion spoke much to me of the unconditional love of God. This once confused and broken person had found self-acceptance, identity and healing. All this despite the religious taboos and social mores in some societies that deny the integrity of the self for the good of the institution. In stepping out of the mould of cold religious respectability, he had been reborn.

In answer to those who refer to Bible passages as evidence in defence of fundamentalist beliefs, I might again single out Job. He knew that the advice of his friends that God always protects his own and punishes those who oppose him (Job 4.7–11) was wrong (Job 21.1–26). Moreover, in the text God seems to agree with him (Job 42.7–9).

A parishioner once told me after a Sunday morning service that what is wrong with society today is that people no longer take any notice of the Ten Commandments. He reckoned that if these laws were read weekly in every church in the land, then standards of personal behaviour would improve and lawlessness would decline. I thought this to be a rather depressing suggestion. He may be right but what would such authoritarianism do to the human spirit? And what would it do to the gospel of love? For such an understanding of Christian morality and lifestyle wipes out in one stroke the Spirit behind the life, death and resurrection of Jesus Christ. As I understand it, the Sermon on the Mount (Matt. 5–7) was meant to lead us on from the legalism of Mount Sinai[4] into a deeper understanding of the nature of authentic love.

I fear that those who frequently speak in such moralistic terms say more about their own insecurity than they do about the Christian faith. They appear to want the Church to provide them with a book of rules by which they can categorize and condemn those who – in their opinion – are dragging down the standards of society.

Of course, without the structures of civil and criminal law, chaos and anarchy would result. Of course, the Christian faith based on the gospel of love offers a life of peace both to the individual and to society. And we should not forget that human beings have to learn the ways of love within a legal framework and structured society. The Church can influence secular structures of society but its responsibility does not stop here. Its most important role is to work within society to create a new kind of kingdom and new possibilities for human relationships. So within these structures the Church is called to proclaim the Christ who came to show that there is a better way to live: the way of love. As St Paul says, if we feel justified in God's eyes simply because we obey the religious law, then Christ died for nothing (Gal. 2.21).

The historical basis of the view that Judith holds is grounded in a literal understanding of the story of the Fall as told in Genesis 2. Yet we now know there never has been a time in the history of the world when creation was in a state of prefallen perfection. Death, disease and natural evils such as earthquakes have always been an integral part of creation. Moreover, the idea that God should punish successive generations for the mistakes of the first two human beings is nonsense. There is really no need for us to feel guilty about this any more.

Nor is it necessary to feel guilty about refusing the idea that humanity should take all the blame. If we feel we have to take the blame for the blemishes and beastliness of God's creation it will mean that our prayers are going to be devoid of any kind of growth in unconditional love. There is too great a contradiction in saying that God created human beings with free will but that it was they who brought about evil. The God who created the world cannot be absolved from the responsibility of creating at least the possibility for evil.

If I am unable to love myself, I cannot begin to comprehend the love of God. My prayers, while fluent at times, will fall way short of heaven. Like thoughts, prayers devoid of love succumb to the gravity of fallen desires, as Claudius says:

> My words fly up, my thoughts remain below.
> Words without thoughts never to heaven go.
> *Hamlet*, Act III, Scene iii

The result of this ignorance of love is that when we say our prayers, instead of standing in God's presence, we creep and crawl about in abject fear. We are convinced that God will love us and speak with us more for our religious mantras than for the offering of ourselves. We dare not offer ourselves because we don't feel good enough.

To pray according to this understanding of God could mean that like the Israelites in the desert we stay at the foot of Mount Sinai (Exod. 19.12). We are afraid even to touch the holy mountain let alone ascend its slopes that we might meet with God at its summit.

We prefer instead to leave it to Moses-like figures – priestly intercessors – who we like to assume are more worthy than we are, projecting on to them a holiness we long to have. They will carry our prayers, for we dare not even raise our gaze to heaven. We shall never scale this spiritual mountain that should represent our developing prayer life nor shall we see God by this route. This is not because our guilt is really so great nor that God is so distant. It is because in our misunderstanding of how salvation works, we have put ourselves at an insurmountable distance from his healing presence.

Judith interprets inward goodness and purity in terms of faultlessness rather than the gradual integration of herself into truth. As a result she is blind to the love around her. She prays for help and understanding but they will never come until she learns to accept herself. She prays in vain to know the presence of God in her suffering because she cannot bear to be as yet in the presence of herself. Instead of being the place where she is set free, the Church becomes her prison.

If we agree with her picture of God, then, like Adam and Eve, in the presence of God we will be afraid to be naked (Gen. 3.9–12). We will prefer to hide because our guilt has not been cleansed but rather reinforced by some well-intentioned but misplaced ministrations of the Church. So instead we try and impress others and even God with our *gnosis*, our knowledge of the spiritual life, rather than trying to live it. Many of us have been brought up to hide behind a tradition that, instead of leading us into his presence, keeps us at a respectful distance from God. We pray for help but we are too afraid to commit ourselves to explore, experience and enlarge our grasp of the way of love. To pray 'Thy will be done' in this context, therefore, becomes to some extent a denial of our own humanity rather than its fulfilment. If our prayers are going to lead us to that place where we can find the peace of God among the injustices of this life, we have somehow to find a way to align our will with his, for 'Sanctity does not consist merely in *doing* the will of God. It consists in *willing* the will of God.'[5]

We need to affirm first of all that the concept of the guilt of humanity did not form part of the original body of church teaching. It is sin that separates us from God rather than guilt. Here sin refers to that kind of self-centredness that prevents us and others from growing and developing as we are meant to. The consequence of the Fall of humanity was that the nature of relationships – those between human beings and between them and God – was distorted and often fractured. Humanity needs the help, rather than the judgement, of God to put this right.[6]

In this context, the priority of the mission of the Church is not to make us feel guilty but to teach us how to rebuild relationships. It is not simply ironic, therefore, but shameful that relationships within the Church are generally speaking so impoverished.

My starting point is therefore substantially different from Judith's. I begin with a belief that we are created by a God of love and made in his image (Gen. 1.26–27; 9.6). Here I can affirm that humanity is fundamentally good and worthy of love and praise rather than biased towards evil, frequently worthy of condemnation and consequently riddled with guilt.

Nevertheless, I have to accept that guilt is central to human experience. How I interpret this within my relationship with God, however, will determine much about how I perceive his love operates.

It is undeniable that feelings of guilt develop in human beings from a very early age. According to Freud, they can originate from failures at the potty-training stage when a child seeks the approval of those she or he respects and relies upon. Alternatively, these feelings may have crept into the collective unconscious as described by Jung at some time in the past, forming part of our psychological inheritance and exerting a strong influence upon our experience of ourselves.

Whatever their origin, the Church can either use these feelings of guilt to manipulate its membership – as it has frequently done in the past – or it can help to bring them to the surface and deal with them in a positive way that promotes the healing of the human spirit.

Having been brought up to feel guilt over even minor misdemeanours, I believe that the religious structures of the Church have often only served to reinforce my sense of lack of self-worth. When I suppress my guilt out of a desire to be loved and affirmed by others within the Church, I begin to hide my faults. I therefore compound my guilt and lose touch with my inner self.

Then I begin to relate to others as someone I think they would want me to be, rather than as myself. They, in their turn, trying to come to terms with their own guilt, do the same. As a consequence, the person I am is very different from the one I project. To this add society's expectations – together with cultural conditioning and the perceived need for conformity – and we can see why we have so many problems in confronting the truth. When Jesus told us to have faith, he meant us to have faith in ourselves.

So whenever the Church confirms our false understanding of human nature, it accelerates the process by which we lose touch with our inner selves. It is not long before we convince ourselves that we are unlovable both to our fellow human beings and to God. Then the being of God becomes increasingly remote.

Instead of being the community of the new humanity, of the integrated self and relationships, Christians can become a community of institutionalized pain and guilt. Instead of being the means by which we achieve freedom, the Church becomes the cause of our spiritual depression.

Tragically, for many the manner in which we do things becomes more important than who we are. Authentic love is superseded by law. We have forgotten that this is exactly the situation Jesus came to reverse.

For there is no room for fear in a loving relationship: 'There is no fear in love, but perfect love casts out fear; for fear has to do with punishment, and whoever fears has not reached perfection in love' (1 John 4.18).

God's will and growing through it

Let us move on from Judith's picture of God as an authoritarian figure to the description Jesus gave us of him as 'Our Father'. The concept of 'Father' by itself, of course, can be taken in a number of ways. Judith would favour a description of a remote Victorian type of figure who would tolerate seeing me from time to time on the condition I didn't say anything until I was spoken to. But there are other and more creative ways of understanding what Jesus was saying here.

Tom – whose recent and untimely death deprived many of the presence of a godly man – was a dear and beloved friend who could not accept the idea that God is remote and authoritarian. Tom's way of understanding God was through the Aramaic word for 'Father' used in the Lord's Prayer and best translated as 'Daddy'. He explained how using this name could help me understand my relationship with God and receive the assurance that God loves me, is on my side and is deeply involved with every aspect of my life. Above all else, God wants me to mature and take responsibility for my life. I felt greatly encouraged by Tom's approach and wanted to draw closer to my 'Father in heaven', for this is a God I wanted to get to know.

Now, I understand that there are times when mine and my Father's aims for my life coincide, and times when they do not. There will be occasions of great intimacy between us and there will also be times when I will sense that he has withdrawn his presence for my benefit, although he will probably be as close to me as ever. Times when he will know what is best for me although this may not be immediately apparent in what he seems to be doing. Times when God seems to have turned my life upside down in order to take away my false pride: 'As for me, I said in my prosperity, "I shall never be moved." By your favour, O Lord, you had established me as a strong mountain; you hid your face; I was dismayed' (Ps. 30.6–7).

So in contrast with Judith's picture, this one is of a sensitive, loving God who above all wants me to mature in my understanding of his love so that I might reach full maturity of body, mind and spirit.

Here God's ultimate and overriding aim for my life is that I should fulfil my potential. But growth – particularly in the area of wisdom and spiritual stature and love – is not guaranteed. If I live in a totally unchallenging environment the chances are that I would remain a child for ever. And a spoilt one at that.

For if I do not encounter suffering and learn how to deal with it and even sometimes overcome it, how can I grow in stature? How can I learn about life if I cannot face death?

When we are struggling through some crisis there is nothing worse than someone with the best intentions saying 'I know how you feel', when clearly they do not. So how can we become deeply compassionate and understanding in our relationships with others and in our prayers if we have not ourselves suffered? Then we will at least be able to stand empathically by others in their time of need.

I used to ask Tom, though, whether it was right to maintain that not only our prayer life but also the complete fulfilment of human potential can only come through our experience of suffering and hardship? Is it inconceivable that God could have come up with a less painful way of achieving this?

To some degree it makes sense that pain can lead to fulfilment but then not everyone experiences pain and reacts to suffering in the same way. What about the parents of the teenager suffering from a degenerative brain disorder? Can we justify their pain, disorientation and confusion as part of a person-making process? Some parents desperately searching for answers may of course find help in prayerful submission to what they understand to be the overriding will of God. Others will somehow reach another peace by a prayerful intuition concerning the continued existence of their loved ones. These we can only admire and applaud.

Others still, I fear, will want to go on searching, questioning why their beautiful child had to suffer so terribly and miss out on so much. They cannot understand that there is anything logical in suffering as the central part of a person-making process because all they can see is that it has deprived their child of life. They ask why one particular child should be singled out so that others who are involved in the process of his or her suffering might become better – more fulfilled – people. For these people prayer remains a place of anguish rather than peace. They lose the faith they once had and remain broken and bewildered by the brutality of it all.

Moreover, if the world is principally God's workshop for the construction of souls fit for heaven, what am I to say to the 37-year-old divorcee I visited in the parish who was living alone and trying single-handedly to bring up her young son? She suffered constant back pain, at times being able only to crawl across the floor of her living room, as a result of having been involved in two unrelated car accidents. In the first she was sitting in her stationary car when she was hit from behind, the force of the impact throwing her through the windscreen. In the other – having already suffered a damaged back – while walking to the shops she was hit by a car that mounted the pavement.

I have no doubt that on one level the image of God as Father would bring comfort to her. She is his child, after all, and he longs to pick her up and comfort her and help her to regain her life. But dare I tell her that one of the reasons this Daddy-God has put her through this is to make her into a better person? If I did, it would surely be understandable if her prayers became those not of a better but a bitter person. It seems unfair to deal such a mortal blow to the faith of this Christian woman who can no longer attend church because of the constant pain she suffers.

Jesus rejects the idea that suffering and death are inflicted on people as a result of wrongdoing or that tragedy takes place for the spiritual benefit of others when he refers to the Jewish workers killed when the tower of Siloam – which they were repairing for the Romans – fell on them (Luke 13.1–5).

Similarly, what 'good news' is this person-making process for someone who lives in an area of severe poverty surrounded by unemployment, drugs, violence and the breakdown of family life? Are we supposed to tell him that God loves him and has willingly allowed this to happen? This is in order that he and his neighbours can work through their suffering and discover true moral values? This pill is particularly difficult to swallow when he can see others developing a prayerful relationship with God without experiencing unemployment or poverty or this kind of drug abuse.

I argued with Tom that this description of God as the craftsman of the human spirit maintains the nonsense that God wanted life to be this way. That he creates us healthy and then makes us ill and eventually kills us to make us better. Surely, pictures of mothers from the developing world with no milk in their breasts, clutching their emaciated and dying babies, stands this theory on its head. For what kind of language is this? It is not the language of love. If, as many would say, we have been placed in a soul-making environment set at a distance from our loving Father-God so that all our decisions are made without coercion, why does it appear that some lives are worth more love than others?

What about the story of the boy in North Africa separated from his parents at birth and brought up by a herd of gazelle in the Sahara? He had no chance to grow up and fulfil his divine potential in conversation with God. Instead, he became a member of a herd of animals and was unable either to make contact or communicate with human beings. While this is an extreme example of all kinds of inequalities of opportunity in human life and history, what purpose could there have been in permitting such an unjustified aberration of the divine potential in human nature?[7]

Tom believed that God had created the world as an elaborate environment for a person-making process and that it makes sense to divide history into two. First is the stage when God creates with omnipotent power. This long process – consisting of billions of years of slow and often painful growth – was necessary to produce humanity. The second stage is the age of spiritual growth. After the coming of humanity, with its reflective awareness and ability for free decision-making, God elicits love from people in order to produce fully developed spiritual beings with whom to share life in heaven.[8] Tom would refer me to the words in the first account of creation in the book of Genesis, 'Then God said, "Let us make humankind in our image, according to our likeness"' (Gen. 1.26a) as indicating a two-stage process in the development of human beings. 'Image' here refers to the potential for knowledge of God and relationship with him that is the natural inheritance of all human beings. 'Likeness' refers to that side of our make-up that is intelligent and able to discern matters on a spiritual level. Tom would argue that the 'image' is intact while the 'likeness' has been lost. The story of Adam and Eve is not about actual events that took place. Rather, it is an invented story used to describe how God created the world at a distance from himself. Humanity has to overcome this distance through moral and spiritual development so that our 'likeness' becomes increasingly 'like God'.[9] So life is like being on a spiritual obstacle course that will make us courageous, strong and self-confident – if we manage to finish it, that is.

However, evolutionary theory indicates that the emergence of humanity has come about as the result of one long, continuous process. It is therefore false to divide history into a two-stage process.

While the arrival on the scene of 'homo sapiens' was of momentous importance, its significance is to be understood only in its relation to preceding history. The make-up of humanity today is latent in its antecedent history. (The genetic make-up of a human differs from a chimpanzee's by very little; there is only something like 2 per cent difference between their DNA and ours.) We cannot speak of human nature without remembering our hunter-gatherer ancestors, any more than we can speak of a Christian identity as if it began with Jesus Christ alone.

Many of the ways in which we cause suffering to others today arise out of our biological inheritance from long ago. There is a definite link between the satellite state seeking self-rule, the primitive tribe defending its territory and the group of primates that sees off intruders from its hunting ground.

We are beginning to realize that the potential for the acceptance or rejection of the purposes of love in the higher forms has evolved directly from the potential for order or disorder in the lower forms of life.

Moreover, there is every reason to suppose that God has always acted in the same way through the same processes of evolution, and if there is not some kind of Fall then the history of evolution becomes an enormously time-consuming process. Why did 'homo sapiens' not appear at an earlier stage? And why could God not have found a way to achieve his ends without inflicting pain on the animal kingdom to the degree that he does?

I was puzzled when Tom used to tell me that I have been put in a world where I have been called to discover God and through that discovery to become God-like. For God seems to work too hard to conceal his true nature. And why doesn't everyone who seeks after God find him? And among those who have 'found' him, why are there so many different descriptions and beliefs about what he is like?

While it appears comforting to begin with, Tom's picture of God clearly doesn't work either. While it brings God closer and presents him as deeply loving and concerned about my welfare, I cannot help feeling that this is just another, although more plausible, diversion from the truth. It holds conflicting negative and positive forces together in a subterfuge of normality. It doesn't recognize evil for what it is or what it does to people. Clearly, my understanding of what Jesus meant when he used the image of God as Father is only partial.

So I have to reject Tom's understanding of the Father-God because of the extent of the indiscriminate nature of human suffering. While there are unquestionable benefits that arise when people face and overcome pain, the inflicting of the required amount of pain to obtain the desired results stands in clear contradiction to the love of the Father. The principal Christian prayer which Jesus himself taught is an unequivocal expression of this love. Clearly, I have to find a better understanding of this

Father. Sadly, I cannot continue my discussions with Tom. I didn't realize how ill he was. He didn't tell me and I didn't visit. So I move on without him.

He would understand that, as my prayers increasingly lead me to the pursuit of the processes of love, I cannot stop now. For my prayers involve me in the lives of the disfigured, crippled and marginalized. On their behalf as well as my own, I have to see why the processes of life – in which we are all engaged to some degree or other – are like this. When in their suffering they ask me how to pray, I need to know how to reply without having to cross my fingers behind my back. My desire to live in harmony with the Divine Spirit of creation forces me to develop my understanding of how these prayers fit, or do not fit, into the purposes of God's love.

Again, the question is not so much to do with the personhood of a father figure in the sky above but about the nature of parenthood. My prayers are the place where love is met, relationships moulded and new life is born, nurtured and blessed. But if this is to be the case, there also has to be a relocation of God within the mess that is me and everyone else too.

Before I can begin to understand the will of God at a graveside, I have to understand that he loves me for the person I am. As Simone Weil says, 'God's love for us is not the reason for which we should love him. God's love for us is the reason for us to love ourselves.'[10]

Investing in creation

Where do we go next? To whom should our prayers be directed? By now we are becoming very down to earth with God. But does this mean we are denying him his divinity? Or are we rediscovering it? For it seems that it is in the continuum of existence and the relatedness of God in all things and all things in God that we will find a viable response to the problem of evil and suffering.

This continuum became almost tangible for me one day when I was looking at the fossil of a dragonfly larva (*Libellula doris*) from Piedmont, Italy, that was 18 million years old. The larva that had once carried within itself the potential to produce and display the most intricate beauty had been caught in mid-stride. It had somehow been denied its opportunity of fullness of expression in which it would, in its own way, have given glory to the Creator God who in the first place had caused it to exist.

Though it had died millions of years ago, the larva was still able to 'speak' of its life to those who would stop, see, reflect and learn. So it was that, in a creature so small and apparently insignificant, I began at long last to come to terms with the precarious nature of life.

The beauty of this fossil made me see that if there is such a significant potential in the larva of a dragonfly, how much more there must be in the possibilities of human life. Yet amid all the possibilities for growth and development, there are as many if not more influences and hazards that can so easily fossilize a person's right to fulfil their potential or the opportunity to love freely and know true love returned.

One composer is fortunate to live in a time of peace, attend college and write musical scores that are admired around the world. Another is conscripted into the army to die in futile trench warfare. The world does not get to hear the unwritten symphonies in his heart. One young woman from a loving and balanced family background falls in love and happily embarks on married life. Another is brutally raped and cheated for ever of the experience of love without fear.

If God really did create the potential for beauty at all levels of life, and is also responsible for creating at least the possibility of evil, I need to understand evil and suffering as both positive and negative features of creation. Moral awareness and spiritual progress can arise out of pain and hardship, but frequently the only result is bitterness and despair. So I need to find out why God holds together a creation that is both beautiful and amazingly intricate, but also grotesque and frightening, in an apparently haphazard way that produces great faith and hope and also cynicism and religious fatalism.

Here sin – understood as my refusal to grow into the person God is calling me to become – is not about breaking religious tradition and law. Sin has more to do with making false divisions between myself and my environment, myself and other human beings, myself and nature, between sacred and secular, God and the world, for sin is a word that describes a general condition of alienation from God in which we worship ourselves.[11] It is overcome by the discovery that God is truly the centre and source of all life.[12]

If this sin is the consequence of falling out with God, redemption consists of relocating God in all things and in particular rediscovering the presence and purpose of his love in creation. This will not be an easy task as good and evil seem to be so entwined at times that it is difficult to tell one from the other.

God suffers, too. Not just as a grieving parent who looks on but as the core participant in the cosmic drama. This is most clearly seen in the cross where the omnipotent God of creation reveals the extent of his voluntary self-limitation as he shares responsibility for life with humanity in Jesus Christ.

I can also see this idea in the Old Testament account of the flood story, which is probably a combination of two stories, one written perhaps in the tenth century BC, the other in the sixth or fifth century BC. At the end, the account of the promise never to flood the world again as a reaction to humanity's sinfulness reveals an understanding of a God who does not intervene in human history to award prizes or punishments. In the first account of creation in the Old Testament, God is clearly understood to share his powers of creativity, thereby giving to humanity the opportunity to hasten or retard his creative purposes (Gen. 1.28–29).

So God is not only the first cause, he is also working alongside me. And he is actively engaged within the processes of creation to bring about the fulfilment of his love. Suddenly I feel a sense of awe, not at the majesty of God, not out of respect for his omnipotence or out of fear of his judgement, but because of the nature of his proximity, because I have come to realize that this is not a prayer of fatalistic submission. Nor is it a prayer for divine miraculous intervention. It is much more than this. It is more than anything about realizing how close he is to me and I am to him. He and I pray, laugh, cry, live and die together.

It is at this point that I find myself drawn into the life of the Trinity. No longer is this a theological construct external to myself but something that is central to the experience of my personal growth and development.

> This is what the spiritual life, at its deepest, really means: not merely 'believing' in God, or even 'worshipping' God, but living and dwelling *in* God. We are no longer mere 'followers' of Christ, we live in Christ, sharing in his relationship to the Father, being 'sons' as he is Son, through the Holy Spirit.[13]

When, therefore, I pray to my loving Father in heaven 'Thy will be done', this is a prayer about my relationship with God. To pray in this way is inevitably to become involved in the progress of creation and the purposes of the life of God within it. God has given me a share of his responsibility for creation and therefore a share in his life. I can no longer regard the world as a playroom for God. Nor in creation is it just humanity that matters. Every part of creation has been forged by Divine creativity and is fused by his presence. Everything, therefore, has intrinsic worth and significance, for God is himself in this creation to such a degree that he is aware of the death of even a small and apparently insignificant bird (Matt. 10.29). Clearly,

God has invested himself in his creation so I have also to invest myself in it if I am to find the Way through.

Elie Wiesel, in the haunting record of his childhood in the death camps of Auschwitz and Buchenwald, tells of the horrifying execution of a young boy. Elie and his fellow prisoners were made to march past three victims who had been hanged. The two adults, being heavier, were dead but the lighter boy took more than half an hour to die. As he passed in front of the boy he heard someone behind him asking, 'Where is God now?' and Elie 'heard a voice within me answer him: "Where is He? Here He is – He is hanging here on this gallows. . . ."'[14]

My prayer amid my experience of suffering begins with myself, but not because I have immense power to cause or relieve suffering in the world, nor because I wish to escape judgement or grow in spirit. While these would be laudable prayers in themselves, my prayer has first to locate the love and presence of God in my life. Having thus located God, I need next to understand what I am doing with this love and what it is doing with me. For if I place God somewhere other than he is, maybe for all the right reasons, my prayer – while meeting a need – is unlikely to do justice to the relationship I am meant to enjoy.

When I begin to explore this love I start to comprehend the darker side to my nature, where it comes from and how it operates. For I feel deep down that it is not only God who is hanging on the gallows of the concentration camp. I am, as well. Or, at least, that part of me that yearns for the triumph of peace and love.

What is more revealing, however, is that while I lament the frustrated purposes of Divine love in the victim, in my greater awareness of who I am, casting off the mask of innocence, I find myself as the executioner, too.

3

Falling out of love

This urge, wrestle, resurrection of dry sticks,
Cut stems struggling to put down feet,
What saint strained so much,
Rose on such lopped limbs to a new life?

Theodore Roethke, 'Cuttings'[1]

Seeing

I sometimes come across those who like to deal in theological certainties and thereby seek by many subtle means to control the relationship others have with God. In these circumstances, thinking for yourself is not encouraged. Asking awkward questions can cause others to regard you as a heretic.

The danger here is that church people adhere to all kinds of core beliefs without ever really understanding them. We use the terminology without unpacking its meaning for our generation. As a result, we can end up speaking a language that few inside the community of faith really feel at home with and those outside find largely unintelligible.

I am not suggesting that the mystery of the Christian faith and the depth of its spiritual tradition should in any way be watered down. I do believe, however, that if the way in which we deal with this tradition reduces our capacity to find the Father-God within ourselves, we need to find new ways of unpacking the truth. Thankfully, we seem to be more tolerant today of different views of the gospel as the Church continues to celebrate the many faces of Christ that are found in different societies.[2]

Jesus speaks about the truth setting us free (John 8.32) and how the Spirit of God is indefinable and unrestricted by religious practice (John 3.8). It seems to me, therefore, that when the Church gives the impression that it can confine Christ within an ecclesiastical tradition, and when the institution seeks its own survival above everything else, it has forgotten that the God she seeks to reveal belongs to the world. We forget that it was in the frustration of the purposes of the love of God in the world – not in the Church – that things went wrong in the first place.[3] We also believe that God 'sent' his Son as one whose life would reveal the nature of authentic love throughout both creation and eternity. Some might argue that to understand Jesus primarily in terms of his unique revelation of authentic love is to turn away from historical revelation and indulge in spiritual sentimentality. But nothing could be further from the truth.

Our thoughts and words need to make sense. There needs to be a coherence about them that is Christ-like. Yet we must realize that all our words and even our thoughts cannot begin to capture the reality of God even if that were our intention. We should use them with great care, warily even, in the presence of what is essentially Uncreated and Unknowable. A famous theologian of the sixth century put it like this:

> There is no speaking of it, nor name nor knowledge of it. Darkness and light, error and truth – it is none of these. It is beyond assertions and denials of what is next to it, but never of it, for it is both beyond every assertion, being the perfect and unique cause of all things, and, by virtue of its pre-eminently simple and absolute nature, free of every limitation, beyond every limitation; it is also beyond every denial.[4]

In this sense we regard Christ primarily in terms of his relatedness to and revelation of the Divine love of the Creator operating within creation. We find that this provides us with the Way to begin to understand the spiritual power or energy that holds life together. Moreover, if the crucifixion of the God of love was brought about by the frustration of love's purposes, it is crucial that our response to the gospel causes us to delve deep into the processes of love that affect our deepest sense of being. This will inevitably take us beyond both the physical and the temporal to the source of prayer itself within the human heart. Having been very much within the Church's ministry for 27 years, I am not ashamed to say that that I am now only just beginning to discover the meaning of Christ for myself. As I have moved from protest to prayerful contemplation, it is as if I have had my sight restored. Like the man who was born blind and healed by Jesus, I can now begin to make out new shapes defined by light and shadow (Mark 8.24). And the more I develop my understanding of prayer, the more my vision improves. Perhaps this is the kind of change of heart that is required before we can see Christ.

So, having moved from the language of protest to that of contemplative prayer, I can speak of the heart as the meeting place of God.

The human heart is a physical organ used to pump blood and oxygen through the body. To speak of heartfelt prayers, however, does not mean that we are moving from reality to fantasy. In trying to give voice to the language of love – which is the language of the heart – writers of faith and vision within the Judaeo-Christian tradition have often used symbols in both myth and mystery to convey the truth that has been revealed to them. It is important we recognize this if we are not to become confused.

The myth, of course, is a form of writing used to express the how and why of life. It is intrinsic to faith stories from societies around the world. It is a legitimate way in which humanity has sought to understand and somehow describe the existence of God in terms of creation and human life.

There are instances of the incorporation of Middle Eastern myths from neighbouring countries in the religion of Israel. There is evidence of this in both Old and New Testaments and their existence does not in any way invalidate the truth they are meant to convey. By writing in the form of myth we can express otherworldly matters using pictures and concepts from our experience of this world.

Myths are intrinsic to spiritual development. We use them not purely to theologize about the existence of God but particularly as we try to make sense of what we feel and touch, our tangible experience of this world. Mystery is another tool we use to communicate what is essentially incommunicable.

Dr Sheila Cassidy – who suffered severely when she was arrested and tortured for treating a wounded revolutionary in South America, and who subsequently worked in the hospice movement – writes that there are at least two approaches to suffering. Either you can treat it as a problem in purely logical or rational terms, for example in the care of the sick and suffering, or you can approach it in terms of mystery that asks, for example, 'Why me? Is God putting me to a test?'[5] Mystery here refers to a spiritual truth – invisible and intangible – that can only be understood by faith either in oneself or in God or both. The only way I can access this mystery is by self-surrender and spiritual contemplation. Then I can grasp its meaning. As Theodore Roethke says, 'I recover my tenderness by long looking.'[6] For 'only to our intellect is he incomprehensible: not to our love'.[7] Contemplative prayer, in this sense, involves more than the ability to 'see' God, the world and myself in a new and interrelated manner. For once we can 'see' what is essentially invisible, we can reach out and be touched by this Divine love.

This is why Jesus said to his disciples, 'To you it has been given to know the secrets of the kingdom of God; but to others I speak in parables' (Luke 8.10). It explains his frustration with them when they did not understand because while their minds were alert, their hearts were hardened. So, while having eyes, the disciples were unable to see and having ears they were unable to hear (Mark 8.18). In other words, they could see and hear Jesus but they were still out of touch with him. Later on, following his resurrection, they would learn how to see and hear in a prayerful encounter that enabled them to keep in touch with Christ even when he was not physically present with them.

Religious people often speak of seeing or hearing God. These experiences form part of our intuitive senses when used and understood in a Godly kind of way. But God reveals himself most powerfully through touch and feeling. Visual and auditory senses are less reliable. So our seeing and hearing God naturally leads us to be able to touch or be touched by him and to make sense of that touch when we feel it. On the road from Jerusalem to Damascus, Paul was blinded by a bright light and he heard the voice of Jesus challenging his hatred of Christians. We mistakenly think that Paul was converted somewhere along this road when in fact it was following the touch of Christ that Paul was baptized. While in Damascus, Ananias was told by the Lord in a vision to go and find Paul, or Saul as his name was then. But it was only when Ananias laid his hands on Paul that the touch of God was both given and received. As a result, the scales fell off Paul's eyes and Ananias was able to help him see God's forgiveness for his life.

Contemplative prayer is therefore not only about being able to see God in the world and the world in God. It is about being able to see, and, because we can see, to reach out and touch Christ in friend and neighbour and in and through creation. Thomas, the disciple, saw the Risen Christ and wanted to touch him and Jesus actively encourages him to put his hand in his side (John 20.24–29). In the previous chapter I described how the fossil of a dragonfly larva 'spoke' to me of the risky processes of love. But in holding that rock, I knew I was touching something no longer ordinary or even extraordinary, but somehow divine. Just as the disciples had to leave behind much of what had become their religious tradition in order to follow Christ, so in a similar way have I.

The Church as a human institution can never be an end in itself. It can only point to a horizon beyond itself. When we focus predominantly on its survival, we are preventing it from fulfilling its function. So while I find unhelpful many of the ecclesiastical structures with which I am involved, it has been by working with and through them that I have reached this place of healing. But I have not earned this ability to see into the human heart by my protest or earnest works of religion or indeed by any goodness or moral superiority. For struggle and protest are good in that they help us escape ideas and 'ologies that oppress us. But we misuse them when we use our theology to try and control others and even God. None of us, no matter how hard we try by amassing finances and facelifts, can control our lives. But within the parameters of love and the largesse of our hearts, we can own our lives in the sense that we can take responsibility for them as gifts of God. Any contemplative insight I may now have into the condition of the heart – the place of prayer and the touching place of God – comes as a gift from the Spirit of God into the mess that is me. This is a gift I must cherish and give to others. It is in this kind of giving that we receive the life of God. As a consequence, I am learning how to love again. For the God of love is known best by love. So instead of struggling, I must now make room within my heart for God to love me back to himself.

Contemplative existence, therefore, as Thomas Merton writes,

> is a sign of the goodness of God, and it enables us to believe more firmly in His goodness, to trust in Him more, above all to be more faithful in our friendship with Him . . . But do not be surprised if contemplation springs out of pure emptiness, in poverty, dereliction and spiritual night.[8]

All this makes me find a kindred spirit in Jacob whose story is told in the book of Genesis. (I sometimes feel that I have more in common with those who live outside the family of the Church than with those who are within it.) Jacob found that the traditional and hierarchical set-up of his family left no space for his creativity. His elder brother inherited the lot. Jacob had no room and no rights. He had to live constantly in the shadow of his brother. By protesting and taking the birthright that he believed should have been his as much as his brother's, he was forced to leave.[9]

In a similar way, society in general has moved away from the Church family whose love threatens to stifle rather than to develop its spiritual inheritance. Like Jacob's father, this family has also stuck too rigidly to inherited patterns of behaviour that are now considered to be out of touch with the needs of the individual. As a result, many have decided to take ownership of their own spiritual journey which they see as their right from birth. Turning their back on tradition, they have forged out into unknown territory in search of their own identity and to find a purpose in life beyond the material and mundane. The pain of rejection and personal pride are likely to keep followers of Christ inside and outside the traditional Church apart. In time, I believe, they will reunite, as did Jacob and his brother Esau in a place beyond Penuel (Gen. 33.1–14). But this will only take place when both are prepared to admit their mistakes and meet in a spirit of reconciliation in a desert place which neither can claim as their own.

Unwittingly, therefore, and primarily as a result of a strong desire to be allowed to grow up and gain ownership of my life, I have grown tired of the convention that once provided me with security. So I have walked away from those within the family of faith that brought me up. While I remain within the Church, I find myself in a desert place. Although at times I feel alone and isolated, at least I can now sleep untroubled by those who threaten my sanity and spirituality by the naivety of their answers.[10]

Here I discover that the house of God does not consist primarily of gathered congregations centred on Sunday Christianity. The Church, instead, consists not only of the traditional organization but also of that family of faithful people who have come away from any household that lives by inauthentic love. For these exiles know that in order to discover and live by the truth of God in Jesus Christ, they have to move on.

In this sense the Church is not an ark that has been left high and dry on the moral high ground of its own choice while the rest of the world gets on with life at ground level. Instead it is the corporate life of those who live by the Spirit of Christ as the one who gives meaning to the pursuit of God within human society and institutions.

As Jacob set up a stone that he had used as a pillow as a sign of his re-awakened awareness of the presence of God, so in the dawn of my desert place I also signal that it was here that my dreams of faith came true. For here at long last – bared of all pretence and being now only myself – I have stumbled across the gate of heaven (Gen. 28.17). Truly, the Lord is in this place and I did not know it.

Loving

When wrestling with the problem of evil I had expected God to conform to the laws of justice as I thought they should be administered. And I was hurt when he didn't. Yet I sense that when my heart was broken God was able to love me all the more. So if it is in my heart that I meet with God, I must offer it to him. For unless I make this sacrifice of love, the pain will undoubtedly return, and, if it does, this time it may break my heart for ever.

If I allow anyone or anything to divert me from this, my past confusion will be doubly confused. And then I will be in that hell where it is impossible to make any connections at all, let alone find integration for my life within God and his life within me.

I can recall once having a sense of this confusion at a time in my life when I was unable to make any sense of my surroundings. I remember looking down at my hands and seeing them involuntarily tighten into half fists so that they resembled the claws of some ferocious animal. As I looked up, I realized I wanted to use these talons to climb a high wall in front of me. I looked around and while I could see clearly, nothing made any sense as I increasingly lost touch with my surroundings. While I could see trees, my mind was not registering them as such. It was as if someone had cross-wired my brain. The result was chaos rather than harmony. It was a terrifying experience – seeing but not being able to make any sense of what I could see.

My environment threatened me with an anarchy of meaningless and discordant images. I felt completely dislocated. I was unable to relate to anything or anyone. The inside of my head was full of chaos and there was nowhere to go to get away from it. Living like this is hell. Self-annihilation becomes the only way out. But lacking any reasonable orientation you cannot dispatch yourself. So you feel helpless while your demons scream and laugh at you.

Somebody made me lie down and called a doctor. When he arrived, he leant over to ask how I was. 'Help me, I'm going mad,' I shouted, grabbing him and pulling him towards me with such force that I tore one of the buttons from his coat.

Fortunately this chaos in my mind – caused by an adverse reaction to some medication I had been given to help me sleep during a difficult and stressful time – did not last long. But its memory has remained with me. Through a changed state of consciousness, this temporary experience of chaos has helped me to understand what it must be like to feel that you are out of the reach of God. There is no such place, of course, but we can sever our links with God to such an extent that we can only live in senseless deprivation of the love he offers. When we do this, our lives descend to various depths of meaninglessness.

I am convinced that if I can learn to live in harmony with God, I shall have the opportunity to integrate into my life my body and soul, my heart and mind, and also earth and heaven. I also sense that when I exclude myself from the love of God, I begin to encounter hell on earth. Instead of love, meaning, community and life, I experience disorder, meaninglessness, loneliness and ultimately death.

These are the two realms in and around which our lives revolve. There are no others. Heaven and hell exist inside us. They are contingent to our approach to life. We can share or inflict them on ourselves and others. Unfortunately, living an honest life does not necessarily mean that we will be left alone to get on with love. What is more, most people in the sinful world are honest, but they know that in order to survive – to put bread on the table – they sometimes have to compromise their love within the society in which they find themselves. But hell always beckons those who – unwittingly or not – end up giving tribute to Caesar by surrendering their allegiance completely to human institutions and agendas (Mark 12.13–17). And we can be quite ingenious at times in the way in which we can convince ourselves that heaven is actually hell, and vice versa. So I must continue in this contemplative prayer of love that touches my heart with the heart of God. For it will not only lead me to see God in creation but also draw me on to know and experience his love. Without it, I will continue to struggle to make connections and to recognize the patterns of love in the world that ultimately – among the pain and confusion – hold it together.

Beauty where you least expect it

Although I am not much good at it, I enjoy gardening. The fulfilment I feel when growing my own vegetables or arranging an attractive multi-coloured flowerbed goes beyond the mere satisfaction of hunger or the aesthetic delight of a well-ordered garden. Like countless others, I have experienced that inner satisfaction that comes from the knowledge that I am co-operating with nature to try and ensure that harmony prevails.

It was in the garden one day that the most unlikely area caught my attention, helping me to make connections and to recognize the patterns of love in a very special way.

It was not the beauty of a rose, the intricacy of a cobweb or the incandescence of a tree in autumn leaf that caught my eye. Instead, it was the compost heap. It was a mound of decayed lawn clippings intermingled with old potato peel, uprooted weeds and goodness knows what else.

It was not attractive at all. In fact, it was a mess. There were no colours to catch the eye. If the various shades of brown reminded me of anything, it was of death. Yet as I contemplated the unlikely spiritual possibilities of a rubbish heap, I discovered a powerful fertilizer for my faith.

I suddenly saw, revealed in the so-called rubbish, three vital aspects of the nature of created existence which are to be found everywhere in this planet. And not just in the natural world either, for they are also found in humanity.

First, I could see that there is order. The plants, shrubs and trees in my back garden grow on the whole according to their genetic make-up. This takes place over a 12-month cycle that is largely predictable. When I neglect to push the mower back and forth the grass continues to grow, reacting to the patterns of weather according to the seasons in an observable and predictable manner. When cut and stored the grass immediately begins a process of breakdown and death.

Second, I could see that my rubbish heap bears evidence of disorder. In addition to the grass there is a pile of cuttings from some roses. If I want the rose to produce its best flowers and to function most economically, I have to prune it regularly. Therefore the same processes that produce beauty which I can admire also produce a distortion of life which then becomes life threatening. Successful growth requires successful culling by natural or human means to sustain and strengthen life. Here, paradoxically, life depends upon death. Or life is sometimes balanced by death as death is sometimes balanced by life. We can see this elsewhere in dense forests where the bigger and stronger trees keep the light from smaller ones. We can also observe this in the way some animals fight one another to secure the best hunting or grazing pastures. And we can see it in the determination of individuals and nations to secure the best natural resources for their own survival.

Third, I could see the most unexpected and remarkable signs of new life. These in a tangle of discarded branches separated from those I have chosen because of their beauty to be productive, used and admired. For in among the contents of the wheelbarrow at some time or other I must have discarded some flowers or plants. These had reseeded themselves away from the manicured lawn and the tidy flowerbeds. Suddenly, and most incongruously, in among the browns and blacks of death, I could see the brightly coloured vigour of life. So, emerging from the refuse stands a flower as intricate and worthy of admiration as any other in the garden. I had not tended this seed with great deliberation, care and nurture. I had discarded it, cut it out and thrown it away. Yet refusing to succumb to the processes of death, it continued to produce life.

Looking further I realize now that this quest for life – and the refusal to give in to anything that threatens it – is present at every level of created existence and in many different ways.

Wherever we look – even in the most apparently hopeless of places – there is a power for life and fulfilment that refuses to be overcome. Not only in the world of nature but also in the world of human endeavour. And when humanity, for example, tries to impose restrictions on the natural power for life, the created world fights back with immense strength. The runway of the disused air force station – from which Vulcan bombers once thundered into the sky carrying weapons with nuclear capability in the Cold War – rapidly succumbs to the grass which eventually grows through and cracks open the concrete. And, perhaps more poignantly, every year on 11 November we remember the poppies that emerged from the blood-soaked mud of Flanders Field.

This 'drive' for the triumph of life amid chaos and the instincts of death lays bare the all-embracing central process of the sanctification of creation. Sadly, this has often been limited in its representation by the Church to hagiographies of human endeavour alone.

As I look at this little miracle of life on the rubbish heap, I can now see that *the very fabric* of the world contains not only order and disorder, balance and imbalance, but also an irrepressible drive for resurrection. Life from death. This earth is not some perfectly peaceful Eden-like environment which humanity has messed up. Rather, creation is itself by nature the crucible in which we seek to discover identity and meaning.

Now I can see how the constituent parts of reality fit together in the unlikely context of love. Life is untidy, unjust and frequently unfair, but, through what can at times appear to be hopelessness, imbalance and injustice, the purposes of love are to be found. Where there is disfiguration and death there is also an inbuilt drive for transfiguration and life.

Driving, thrusting, reaching out, seeking fulfilment, there is an energy at the heart of creation that carries it relentlessly onward, just as there is energy in the heart of my life that constantly drives me on to make sense of my faith and compels me to learn how to love. As John Hunt observes, 'Good religion works from the bottom up, not the top down. It grinds away in the tiny daily events, the moments of realization, through which matter evolves into love.'[11]

What is more, the revelation of the garden rubbish heap led me to understand that the level of self-awareness that humans have – where we work out our identity and relationship with

God – is not supposed to separate us from the Spirit of creation. Our interests have to be worked out wherever possible in co-operation rather than in collision with creation.

My heart is where my desire for prayer and communion comes from. Hitherto I thought my desire to find answers, justice and a kind of loving that made sense came solely from my mind. And I have to be aware that the mind is also where the desire for dominance and control can also create divisive intentions. The general law of nature is the domination of the weak by the strong. Knowing more about prayer and communion means that I must rise above the law of nature by choosing love. In this sense, it is better that the heart rules the head.

So this desire for spiritual union is initiated not by me but by God. It is a consequence of the life of the Spirit within me seeking its natural union with the Spirit of creation, the Spirit of the universe, which is at the heart of God.

God is already within me, at my centre, in my heart. My desire to have a heart beating in time with the heart of God is also his desire, too. While religious rituals help us to gain access to God, I sense that, most important of all, we need to learn to breathe more deeply. For God in his goodness seeks only my spiritual, emotional and physical integration into the fullness that is Him. This God-breathed dust which is me finds ultimate meaning only within the life of God.

So this prayer in which I am sharing is but a recognition and sharing in the prayer of God within me and creation. It is to do with sharing the life of God, who I am in him and who he is in me.

This means that I cannot pray in any way that does not regard my body and spirit as a unity within creation. The aim of prayer is not to release the spirit from the body but to put me back in touch with creation. It is about my recognition of my spirit and body as an integrated whole – as a 'temple of the Holy Spirit' (1 Cor. 6.19) in the words of St Paul – where the God of creation in Christ comes to dwell.

So we live, work and pray for the healing not only of ourselves but of creation, too. For 'this idea of cosmic redemption' – which we call universal redemption – is, according to Orthodox belief, 'a right understanding of the Incarnation'. Christ took flesh, thereby beckoning 'the redemption and metamorphosis of *all* creation – not merely the immaterial, but the physical'.[12]

This is why it makes no sense to say 'love the sinner but hate the sin'.[13] For we cannot separate the effect of a self-centred lifestyle from the way in which a person is physically present within the world. In the incarnation Christ redeemed the whole person. The body is sanctified with the spirit.

Redemption is about how we can re-enter the world in a new way – the way of Christ – rather than escaping from its often harsh reality. Although for some who are very sensitive, or for those who have become spiritually sensitized in a specific way, there is a need to withdraw either on their own or in community with others in order to bear the burdens of the world.

But if my prayer is bound up with a universal prayer of love in creation, how do evil and suffering fit into this? Am I going to be led back to that image of God, whom C. S. Lewis once described in his grief following the premature death of his wife from cancer, as a 'Cosmic Sadist'?[14]

Falling out

I have for a long time been fascinated by the life of a man called Origen who was probably the finest theologian of his day. He lived in Alexandria in North Africa from around AD 184–254. He had a brilliant mind and refused to be confined by convention.[15]

He was not unfamiliar with suffering. When Origen was 17 his father was imprisoned for being a Christian, tortured and publicly beheaded. Subsequently Origen was driven by an extraordinary desire to pursue and proclaim the faith. Later on in his life he opened a school in Alexandria, continuing to teach during times of persecution when other Christians went into hiding. He adopted a harsh way of life that was characterized by voluntary poverty, fasting, celibacy and asceticism. Three years after being imprisoned and tortured during the persecution ordered by the Emperor Decius (249–251), he died at the age of 70.

As a radical theologian of his time, Origen was denounced within the Church for his allegorical rather than literal interpretation of scripture. He was not afraid to say that he understood the account of the Fall in Genesis 2 as a myth, and not as historical fact, as was the predominant view of his contemporaries.[16]

Like others, he believed that evil came from the misuse of freedom. But unlike them he saw the original rebellion or Fall as having taken place *before* the creation of this world. He held a highly controversial belief in a pre-cosmic Fall from grace, a separation that took place between the Creator and the created prior to the creation of the world.[17]

Here we can express the sense many feel that just as we believe there is a life beyond this world to which, to some degree or other and in some kind of shape or form, we will go, this life also exists before this world from which, to some degree or other and in some kind of shape or form, we have come. And by 'before' I do not just mean in the temporal sense but also in the sense that it exists, in some sense, outside and alongside the life of this world.

While there are significant overlaps between Origen's thought and that of others in mainstream Christianity, it is not altogether surprising that the reaction of the establishment was to close ranks and reaffirm the historicity of the Fall, a belief which most of us find untenable today.

So, unfortunately, Origen's spiritual insight was buried by the ecclesiastical consensus of the time.

While I would not wish to embrace Origen's scheme in its entirety, his idea of a pre-cosmic Fall shows that – once we have accepted the Bible story of the Fall as myth rather than history – it is possible to think that the origins of evil may have pre-dated the creation of the universe.

You would think that the two principal descriptions of creation in the Bible – found in the first two chapters of Genesis – would contradict such an idea. And you would think that suffering and evil could not be as close to the heart of God as to 'exist' before the physical creation of this universe. For haven't we been brought up with the idea that 'it's all our fault'? Have we not been blind to the lie that creation was somehow perfect except for human sinfulness, despite this notion being contradicted by most of what we know?

However unorthodox this may seem, the idea of some kind of pre-cosmic Fall provides a deeper understanding of the presence of evil not only as we read about it in the second account of creation in Genesis (Gen. 2.4b—3.24), which contains the story of Adam and Eve, but also in the first (Gen. 1.1—2.4a).

We should not forget that these mythological accounts were written by different authors living approximately five hundred years apart, one in Israel and the other in exile in Babylon.[18] Their authors were guided by their spiritual insight to convey deep spiritual truths about those things that cannot be known by the finite human mind. They wrote not as eyewitnesses of the beginning of the world but as those who were trying to make sense of their suffering.

In the first creation story (Gen. 1.1—2.3) we can see that everything was far from perfect from the outset. Instead of being a place where God and human beings might enjoy unbroken fellowship, the earth was a place where something sinister was *already* present. If we look closely, we can see that at the very beginning, God was engaged in a battle to overcome something that was alien to his handiwork.

In Genesis 1.2 we can see in the words 'The earth was without form and void' that it was a completely desolate and inhospitable place. This is emphasized by the words that follow, 'and darkness was upon the face of the deep'. To the early Hebrew mind 'darkness' implied those things that were a threat to life. The presence of the Spirit (*ruach*, also meaning 'wind' or 'breath') moving over the face of the waters signifies the good and creative presence of God seeking order amid the chaos.

The first command God gives is to create light. This indicates that while the darkness was not dispelled completely, it was the prime aim of God to bring it under control so that it might one day be transformed. There is no need for the author to have included 1.2 at all. The creation story makes sense without it. But it was his aim to show that, from the beginning, flawed material had been present in the fabric of the world.[19] That God saw in the end that it was 'good' means in this context, therefore, that he had set in motion all that was required for creation to be redeemed.

A similar picture is given in the second creation story (Gen. 2.4b—3.24) where we read the well-known story of Adam and Eve in the garden of Eden, where even in this apparently idyllic setting evil is already present in the figure of the serpent. While Adam and Eve are placed in a setting of innocence and unbroken harmony with God, they choose to abuse their freedom. Making the wrong choices, they bring about suffering and a disintegration of the Divine–human relationship.

So what are we to make of the 'darkness' in the first story and the 'serpent' in the second? How did they get there and why?

It is quite logical to say that if God created out of his love an environment where he wanted human beings to live by love, this had to be an arena where free decisions could be made. In other words, you cannot make a free decision to choose goodness if this is not balanced by an equal choice for evil.

So the 'darkness' and the 'serpent' stand for the opportunity to misuse the freedom to love that we have been given and also for the consequences of those negative choices.

Saint Augustine, writing in the sixth century, talked of sin and evil in terms of a wilful turning of ourselves from God and as a result we are deprived of goodness. Writing some years later, Maximus the Confessor maintained that misuse of the soul's powers leads to their evil aspects dominating us. So, for instance, the misuse of intelligence results in ignorance and stupidity: 'This being so, nothing created and given existence by God is evil.'[20]

So while the possibility for evil seems alien to the creative purposes of a loving God, we can see that evil surfaces in the rejection of those purposes.

But I still cannot believe that a loving creator God could willingly pre-set his creation and, as a first choice, permit death to prevail to such a demonic degree. It seems that the 'darkness' and the 'devil' are symbols of negative struggle in creation, of a negative energy that seeks to pull down, divert and disfigure rather than build up, harmonize and transfigure. To understand this better, we need to look more closely at the figure of the devil.

The figure traditionally associated with making the wrong choices is the devil or Satan. In him the balance has tipped from life to death regardless of the outcome and consequent suffering. The name Satan literally translated means 'Adversary' or 'Opponent'. I am not suggesting that Satan is either co-equal with God or even necessarily to be understood in personal terms.[21]

This personification of evil in the figure of Satan only became a recognized entity in Old Testament literature at, or after, the time Israel spent in exile in Babylonia, some several hundred years before the birth of Jesus Christ.

During this time there was a cross-fertilization of thought between Jewish, Babylonian and other Middle Eastern cults which referred to a devil figure. And as we are aware, intuitive spiritual insight is not the sole preserve of one culture or generation. For example, the Old Testament notion that human beings were formed out of dust or clay (Gen. 2.7; Job 33.6) is present in Babylonian and Egyptian mythology, while there are stories of a primeval Flood from around the world. In the New Testament, the mythological writings about the end of time are considered to be a blend of Iranian and Jewish thought and the concept of a supernatural birth for the Chosen One of God is not unique to Christianity.

I am not suggesting that because something is myth it cannot be the bearer of truth. Rather, I am saying that the exploration of common mythological form and language can lead – through a process of selection and historical development – to further discoveries about Truth. It is completely reasonable to suppose that by the cross-fertilization of ideas which form the basis of different mythologies, there will, through millennia of spiritual development, one day come a general consensus about life, its origin and meaning. Christians who define themselves by their membership of institutional churches do not hold a monopoly on the Spirit of Christ.

Many, of course, believe for a number of reasons that the idea of Satan in the twentieth century is unworkable. For them, belief in this figure and its attendant demons belongs to a time of pre-Enlightenment ignorance.

> Lucifer expresses our sin, he does not explain it. All that diabolic temptation can supply is motive, or bias; and here the demonic hypothesis is more than superfluous. We have motives and biases in plenty deriving from natural or historical causes. There is scarcely room for Satan to squeeze in any more.[22]

However, we know that there are plenty of examples from the twentieth century – not least in the killing fields of Rwanda, Cambodia and Kosovo – where evil has become personified in devilish behaviour. So much so as to convince the sceptical of the presence not only of the devil but of God as well. Lt Gen. Roméo Dallaire writes:

> I know there is a God because in Rwanda I shook hands with the devil. I have seen him, I have smelled him and I have touched him. I know the devil exists, and therefore I know there is a God.[23]

He didn't meet the devil in traditional guise (horns and pointed tail), but through his contact with demonized human beings he became utterly convinced that he had met him. There are already further examples of this type of Satanic encounter emerging in the twenty-first century.

While in certain circumstances death can produce life – negative forces can hold a creative balance with positive forces – in the world of evolutionary struggle, any such kind of balance is lost when evil becomes demonic. This happens in human beings when evil behaviour is cumulative, when so many related wrong decisions are made – in the mind of an individual or among a group of people together – that there is little likelihood there is anything left that is remotely redeemable.

Returning to the Old Testament, we see that the figure of Satan is alluded to in the writings of Isaiah from the eighth century BC. Here he is understood to have been an adversary both before the creation of the world, in a pre-cosmic setting of perfect harmony, and after the creation of this world.

It was from the harmony of the pre-cosmic setting that Satan fell, being 'cast out of heaven' for some reason which we do not know exactly, but which may be described in terms of self-centred pride or the desire to equal or be greater than the Creator God:

> How you are fallen from heaven,
> O Day Star, son of Dawn!
> How you are cut down to the ground,
> you who laid the nations low!
> You said in your heart,
> 'I will ascend to heaven;

I will raise my throne
    above the stars of God;
I will sit on the mount of assembly
    on the heights of Zaphon;
I will ascend to the tops of the clouds,
    I will make myself like the
        Most High.'
But you are brought down to Sheol,
    to the depths of the Pit.
                (Isa. 14.12–15)

And didn't Jesus also talk about seeing Satan fall from heaven? John, the Apostle, too (Luke 10.18; Rev. 12.7–12)?

Whether or not we consider Satan to be a mythical figure, these brief examples show that in the Hebrew and Greek scriptures and the early Church it was acceptable to comprehend the presence of an evil imbalance in a pre-cosmic setting around the creative heart of God in terms of a wilful turning away from him. An environment of pure love was ruined by arrogance, pride and the desire to work against rather than with God before this world began.

We should add at this point that with our current understanding of the origins of life, we would want to extend this description from a pre-cosmic to a pre-universal setting. So we can assert that from the Big Bang[24] there emerged not only the planet which we inhabit but the universe itself.

Given our knowledge of creation, is there anything more that we can say concerning the balance of love and the imbalance of evil in a pre-universal setting?

Love and the beginning

I feel that I am now in the desert to which I referred earlier. Here my prayers cannot be sustained by the words of others. Underneath this clear and starlit night, I can only seek the Word of creative love. For I cannot pretend that I am the author of such a journey. It is God who keeps challenging me. His spiritual energy seems to move restlessly and ceaselessly over the darkness of my heart.

At times I have wished he would go away and leave me alone. I hated it when he brought his light to bear on me. Faith at first complicates life – often vastly so – before it brings its peace. Darkness wasn't as frightening as the half-light of dawn. Strangely enough, I knew where I was in total darkness. I was used to it. I could not see myself and didn't want to look. But as the light of Christ began to illuminate my life I felt uneasy. In the shadows, my godlessness was coming to light. Terror would take its hold of me again as I realized how I crucified this Christ almost daily by my rejection of his love. I took comfort by telling myself that this body of broken love could never be mended.

I appear to have left a lot of familiar theological landmarks behind. But as the Spirit works increasingly to bring order out of this chaos, I feel I am beginning to rediscover love. But this is a different kind of love from that which I have known.

In a pre-universal setting and as a natural expression of his love, God created free beings capable of a loving response. He sought nothing for them but the highest good. Therefore he was content to take the supreme risk of love. This is to say, first and unconditionally, 'I love you', without in any way coercing a loving response. Authentic love cannot force a loving response from the object of its love otherwise it becomes 'love with conditions'. A child's freedom to respond to his or her parents can be diminished by the child being spoilt, showered with presents or coerced to make the same decisions, adopt a similar approach to life as his or her parents. But this kind of love does not last long, for true love cannot be forced or bought. Therefore love inevitably exposes the lover to the risk of rejection.

So in a pre-universal setting God shared his love with total freedom and without conditions. Of course, an omnipotent God could coerce or command obedience, but he chooses not to in a free, loving relationship. An understanding that a desire to love exists does not necessarily mean a reciprocation of that love. For a free decision can only be made where there is an equally viable alternative to the one that is hoped for.

God's first choice, then, in a pre-universal setting was that he and his created beings should live together in harmony. (The nature of this relationship is pictured very clearly in the story of Adam and Eve in the second account of creation.) Yet God fully realized that if his love was not returned, the result would be a godlessness and evil that would involve much self-sacrifice on his own behalf in the process of restoring harmony and peace.

Therefore, in the precarious and vulnerable activity of the sharing of his love, God is totally responsible for at least the existence of the possibility of evil.

Here where free beings were given the freedom to love, they were also given the freedom not to love. *But here my suffering* – coming as it does as a result of the pursuit of evil alternatives – *is neither primarily or principally a punishment nor a refining fire*, although it can be perceived and 'used' as both by God and myself.

So while I experience evil and suffering in common with my ancestors – although their understanding of it at times will have been very different – I find comfort in the knowledge that God, as a loving parent from the very depths of his being, longed that the possibilities for evil would not be translated into decisions against himself and cause consequent suffering for his creation.

Nevertheless, in a pre-universal setting there came a time when the possibilities for evil were pursued and decisions made against the love of God to such a degree that the original plan was ruined, although not irredeemably so. The result of this pre-universal rebellion was an enormous explosion – a massive dislocation, even a disintegration – of the elements of life, of the environment where God had shared his love prior to the formation of the universe.

Scientific knowledge helps us to understand these elements as having at their centre a kind of creative energy that is the basis of all created reality. This energy now exists in an environment that sometimes assists and at other times hinders its creativity; it reveals balance and imbalance, symmetry and asymmetry. The law of nature is that everything positive has an equal and opposite negative, and we are part of that system. Everything in nature revolves around that balance and equilibrium, although forces are constantly disrupting it.

Following the explosion, while the nature of God himself remained intact, the harmony of relationship he had enjoyed with his created beings became shattered, fragmented and contaminated.

The result of this explosion – or Big Bang – is life known by humanity as the product of aeons of evolutionary growth and hardship.[25]

But because this was a pre-universal Fall and because the love of the Creator was woven through his creation, we can understand how the energy of the basic building blocks – atoms and molecules – of this world are permeated by the energy of the love of God intermingled with the forces of evil. Get the balance right and things turn out OK. Get it wrong and they fall apart. Here Spirit and matter combine. One does not exist apart from the other.

Consequently, the love of God can only be known in a contaminated, alien and often hostile environment. This is why it is at times so difficult to locate and relate to this God of love. Here in creative tension both positive and negative elements usually work together to produce life. At other times the positive overcomes the negative or, tragically, the negative frustrates the positive: 'in 1996 scientists reported the discovery of a gene for novelty-seeking behavior – at the time regarded as a good thing. In 1997, another study saw a link between the same gene and a propensity for heroin addiction.'[26]

As soon as the 'dust had settled' following the Big Bang, the Divine energy or the Spirit of authentic love – which is intrinsic to all the shattered entities both organic and inorganic – began at once in the most primitive forms of life to express its lure for life. We can see this in the way the Divine energy produces order and life from chaos in ever-increasing degrees of complexity.

The aim of this spiritual regeneration is, of course, the eventual reunification of earth with heaven, which Jesus refers to when he teaches his disciples to pray 'your will be done on earth as it is in heaven' (Matt. 6.10). God's primary hope is for creation to return to its Creator. The progress and development of this love and life (for the former gives birth to the latter) has invariably been difficult, costly and painful, based as it is on the acceptance or rejection of the purposes of creative love at every level of created existence.

The history of the world then becomes the history of the growth of the love of God in the face of the evil that pervades everything. In the early stages – and in the basic elements of life today – we can see the history of love expressed in a lure for life, that things should turn out right. In later stages, love emerges through altruistic and kenotic – self-emptying – behaviour in human beings, its fullest expression being seen in the life of Jesus Christ.

In the early stages – and in the basic elements of life today – we can see the history of evil expressed in a lure for chaos, that things should turn out wrong. In later stages, evil emerges through the self-obsessed abuse of power, its fullest expression being seen in those in whom the devil becomes incarnate.

More specifically, among human beings,

> Love's task is to abandon self-defence and go to meet pain and provocation and, despite their impact, to remain unchanged, undiminished and undeterred. Love's task is to confront what keeps another in pain and bondage and,

> by boldness and conquest, to release the prisoner from the powers that afflict him. Love's task is ultimately to confront the source of evil and overcome the terror of his weapon of pain.[27]

Having been cast out of heaven, the devil now represents the bias towards the making of wrong decisions (decisions for death rather than life) in this world. His figure is one of pride and disobedience and, unable in any way to be a creative force, he can only lure away, frustrate and negate the life of love. Each generation meets the devil in different guises but peddling the same old wares. As John Steinbeck reminds us:

> We have only one story. All novels, all poetry, are built on the never ending contest in ourselves of good and evil. And it occurs to me that evil must constantly respawn, while good, while virtue, is immortal. Vice has always a new fresh young face, while virtue is venerable as nothing else in the world is.[28]

We now see the world as a battlefield where victory is to be found in the true expression of the creative love of God over against the power of evil. As St Paul reminds us, 'For our struggle is not against enemies of blood and flesh, but against the rulers, against the cosmic powers of this present darkness, against the spiritual for as of evil in the heavenly places' (Eph. 6.12).

It is also important we are aware that with the emergence of homo sapiens – with its developed level of consciousness together with its potential for 'love without conditions' both for people and for God – the battle has entered a new phase. For the potential for reunification of the shattered entities with their source has taken on a new reality in the reflective awareness and spiritual development of humanity.

This means that, in common with all humanity, we have been given the potential to love as God loves, that is, without conditions. In myself Christ can become incarnate in the world in such a way that, through the deification of my life, heaven and earth are brought another step closer together. So when I pray 'Thy kingdom come, Thy will be done on earth as it is in heaven', I am granted not only the vision but also the power to make this happen. The redemption of creation has now reached a new – and some would say final – phase of Christo-genesis.[29]

Those whose lives negate the fulfilment of Divine love in creation keep me – and all others who seek the triumph of authentic, unconditional love – preoccupied and frustrated today. In their rejection of this love they threaten to turn the life energies of this planet against themselves.

They want the mind to dominate the heart. To use the gifts of creation for themselves. To take power and control over their own destiny – to usurp the resources of the world for the sole end of their self-preservation – at the expense of the fulfilment of others. Their abuse of power becomes most lethal in their threat to mishandle nuclear power and in the use of nuclear weapons. They would take us by another Big Bang all the way back to the beginning again. It is therefore no exaggeration to say that never in the history of the emergence of the Spirit of love have the stakes been higher.

Neither natural nor moral evil in the processes of evolution is therefore willed on humanity *as a first choice decision* in the creation of the world. They are, instead, the tragic result of a pre-universal Fall which has affected and brought pain to the heart of God as well as humanity. And the universe is the arena where love and order battle to overcome chaos and disorder.

So the world is not an environment designed primarily for soul-making, but a bubbling cauldron. Nothing comes into the world ready-made. This is why my present experience of love and my search for God even within the Christian faith is fraught with such difficulty. The history of the world is the history of the progress of love at the expense of evil.

By contrast to any authentic search for meaning within or outside religion we can now see that humanity's abuse of life, its rape of the earth and the threat of possible further use of nuclear weapons threatening a second Big Bang, is nothing other than the wilful turning of humanity's back on the Spirit of creation in the one kind of sin that is unforgivable (Matt. 12.31). Moreover, if we can push the Fall back like this, into a pre-universal setting, we can see also that fall–redemption is not something that just happened once as recorded in the book of Genesis and was put right once and for all through Jesus. Instead, we are beginning to realize that fall–redemption is an archetypal story that describes a constantly repeated – even cyclical pattern – of Divine–human relationships. In human beings, it happens for example whenever we move away from living with nature and instead try to dominate it and abuse it. Then we embark on a culture of greed where the unfair distribution of resources is the end result. When we recognize the error we have made, we promote green agendas and the needs of those we have impoverished.

Fall–redemption is not something to be consigned to history which for ever defines in a particular way how we should believe and live, but is rather a recurring pattern of daily life. For we do not fall from grace once but many times – even constantly – whether it be in our relationships with our friends, spouses, partners or more specifically with God. On the positive side we may describe it thus:

> The fall can be thought of as an evolutionary 'fall upward'. For each evolutionary step there is a cost – and experience of the fall . . . Animal life, human life, cultural evolution, Neolithic culture, urban civilization, the industrial revolution may all have opened new possibilities and brought new freedoms. But each liberation brings new sufferings and new possibilities of enslavement.[30]

Here it is important that we learn from our falls and use each occasion as an opportunity to discover more and draw closer to ourselves, one another and to God. It is here that fallen human beings can grow up.

Fitting the pieces together

So how should we summarize the advantages such a pre-universal Fall myth has over the other responses to suffering which we discarded earlier?

First, while God is responsible for creation and within it for the option of evil as the opposite of pure love, we no longer need to struggle with the idea that God has created the world as it is as a first choice.[31] This is not how he hoped it would be. The world came about as the consequence of the intention of God to love and permit his created beings to live in freedom. This fallen world was always a possibility, but it was not necessary for life to be like this in the first place. There was another, better way. However, this world is the arena we have been given for love to work out its purpose. This is not to say that the devil – that is, the lure to chaos and meaninglessness as opposed to the Spirit who is the lure for life and love – ultimately accounts for there being a world at all. There would have been no possibility of a pre-universal Fall without first the loving creativity of God. The devil has no power to create. He has only the power to negate, to be self-orientated rather than God-orientated, thus producing meaninglessness. Moreover, the devil is unable to sustain such a world because the overall picture of the world's evolutionary growth is one of progress towards greater complexity. So we can still describe creation as being the result of the conscious act of a loving God in that its life is part and parcel of the processes of the sharing of his love.

Second, we can now do away with the picture of God creating the world as an assault course. I once described God as sitting and spectating from a safe distance while telling everyone to scramble over the course in the full knowledge that some would not make it to the end. By contrast, I can now say that while the assault course has been built by the rebellion of others, God longs for everyone to negotiate the obstacles in safety and complete the course. Here God has not erected the obstacles as his first intention; therefore he is able to identify much more closely with the experience of frustration, suffering and pain within every human being.

Third, we can dispense with traditional fall–redemption models of life. The Christian faith is not about devising a process whereby humanity may ingratiate itself into the goodwill of the Divine Being. We have spent too much time in the past seeking restoration and rehabilitation from a guilt that isn't there. We have prayed for an absolution we have not needed.

Instead of being afraid, we can now learn how to become involved with God in the prayer and processes of love in every level of creation. With the advent of humanity, creation becomes conscious of itself and of the Divine potential in every living atom of existence. Christians – and other people of God's Way – therefore become mediators between humanity and the physical universe and between humanity and the sub-atomic world.[32]

No longer do we cower before a severe deity. Instead, as we contemplate the God who is above and beyond and also within and alongside, we feel and observe the energy of his love. To think in this way is to have much more in common with the thinkers and theologians who were involved in the roots of the Christian faith in the Orthodox East.

In this context, the consequences of sin – rather than being seen in terms of inherited guilt – become manifest in my propensity to produce fractured relationships. This is largely due to my genetic bias to put self first and to opt for the 'survival of the fittest', which is a prime example of the inherited mixture of good and evil which we all have to learn to live with.

This is countered now by my prayers that are less to do with being saved from eternal damnation and more about being filled increasingly with the Divine presence. I pray that I might become increasingly incorporated into the Divine energies[33] (but not the Divine essence that I should become a god as well) and achieve union with them in this world and the next.

Irenaeus in the second century said that 'God became man in order that man might become god.'[34] This does not mean that we are meant to try and make ourselves equal with or share in the essential nature of God. In becoming 'god' we share in the Divine energy in creation in such a way that we become 'like Christ'. (To this I shall return in the final chapter.) Christians seek first not to judge or condemn but to affirm the Divine potential in every human being. This involves us in nothing other than a constant and joyful celebration of human relationships. George Fox, the founder of Quakerism, said, 'Walk cheerfully over the world answering that of God in every human being.'

Here prayer describes – sometimes defines – the kind of life we lead. Instead of being something we do on occasions or at certain times, the prayerfulness of our lives is about how much we participate in the Divine life of creation. As part of this prayerful existence, there are likely to be times when we are more specifically at prayer than others; times, for example, when we are 'saying our prayers'. But for the most part and by the grace of God, the life of a Christian becomes itself a prayer of some kind or other.

As we seek thus to participate increasingly in the Divine energies of creative love we resist any kind of over-simplification of the sacramental life. For in this life we do not understand 'spirit' as somehow unconnected from 'matter'. Our spirits do not reside in human bodies as ghosts rattling around in elaborate computers. But while spirit and body are indefinably one they are not finally so in that ultimately the spirit returns to the God who gave it.

There are times – particularly as we go about our daily lives – when we need to be aware of our bodies, using them in a prayerful manner, supporting and sustaining others. And there are other occasions when we will find it helpful to forget about them in prayer, for example when we are in silent meditation or contemplation.

As we increasingly surrender our bodies to God in prayer (Rom. 12.1), both in active and passive mode, we sense his closeness and his transforming love described by St Symeon as follows:

> Completely intertwined with me, he embraces me totally.
> He gives himself to me, the unworthy one,
> And I am filled with his love and beauty,
> And I am sated with divine delight and sweetness.[35]

As time passes, it becomes increasingly difficult not only to discern the difference between spirit and body but also between Divine and human spirit.

The danger, however, is that through a lack of perception we fail to see what God is calling us to become. We have failed to appreciate our significance as children of the Father of creation. This is because we remain subservient to the consequences of human parenthood and parenting. This is the difference between what St Paul calls being descendants of the first and second Adams. '"The first man, Adam, became a living being"; the last Adam became a life-giving spirit' (1 Cor. 15.45).

When we are disorientated by the dysfunctional parenting of Adam and Eve we need to ask again, 'Who is my father or mother?' and by implication 'Who are my brothers and sisters?' (Mark 3.33). For this is not merely a statement about physical identity or genetic origins but about a desire to understand who I am when I am being real to myself.

Recognition of Divine parenthood, in the words of Jesus, is given to those who do the will of their Father in heaven (Matt. 12.50). In other words, to those who are about the process of prayerful godliness.

Fourth, while maintaining a belief in evolutionary theory, the distasteful nature of evil and the fact that it is opposed to the love of God in creation can be addressed. Evil and good do, on occasions, combine to produce a good result in a shattered but developing world. On occasions, evil may even enable further possibilities of love to exist. Yet evil is rooted at its very worst in a source that seeks the negation of the purposes of God. Here God and humanity suffer together in the working out of the ongoing processes of the healing of the world.

The acid test of this pre-universal Fall myth, however, will be in the added meaning this brings to life and faith. The outcome of this will determine whether we have simply pushed the problem of the origin of evil back into an unworkable realm or discovered a way that leads to a greater perception and understanding of the human experience of suffering.

The flower of forgiveness

I realize now that my earlier misunderstanding of God was the result of confusion. It was not a deliberate choice to live an adversarial existence against God. Shadows have for ages been the place where humans tend to live and from where most of us emerge to find a deeper awareness of ourselves and God. But I am not afraid of my shadows any more. I have come to see a God whose love seeks to surface wherever there is life. This powerful creative energy of God within the fallen world seeks not only the completion of the love of God but also the completion of myself as a person of love.

Everywhere I look I can recognize the enormous strength of the operation of the Holy Spirit in its drive and potential for the fullest expression of life at every level of existence. Through medical science and technology, humanity can now work increasingly to nullify the evil lure that takes advantage of the creative risk in all things. This 'divine activity' is indicative of our unique position in creation. Within us the Spirit of love can take on the identity or image of God in the potential we have to promote good at the expense of evil.

The commitment and resilience of the inbuilt spiritual 'lure for life' can perhaps best be seen in the indomitable spirit of humanity. This refuses to succumb to tragedy or pain, or be 'crippled' by disfigurement or dismemberment, displaying an almost unnerving potential to overcome evil with love.

As we have seen in the garden rubbish heap, the best illustrations of this come from the most unlikely situations. As world events make us constantly aware, groups of human beings – whole nations even – can unwittingly end up on rubbish heaps as a result of the political ambitions of others. Sometimes with horrifying results:

> Man is evil,
> I say aloud.
> Man is a flower
> that should be burnt,
> I say aloud.
> Man
> is a bird full of mud,
> I say aloud.
>
> Anne Sexton, 'After Auschwitz'[36]

Considered unproductive or uneconomical to keep because of their perceived ugliness in relation to the manufactured so-called beauty of the dominant ruling class, they are uprooted and tossed to one side. Thought to pose a threat because they are either more or less efficient than those who would wear the crowns of human power, they become a threat to uniform life. Perceived to be a drain on resources, they are consigned to die.

Here, in the most extreme circumstances, a choice has to be made between the lure for life or the lure for death; whether to be a victim of evil or the victor in healing love; whether to contribute to the growth of the Holy Spirit or to give in to godlessness.

Yet out of this degradation, unjust suffering, torture and execution can arise a flower of great beauty. The flower of forgiveness.

This prayer was found on a piece of wrapping paper near the body of a dead child in Ravensbruck concentration camp where 92,000 women and children died:

> O Lord, remember not only the men and women of good will, but also those of ill will. But do not remember all the suffering they have inflicted on us, remember the fruits we have borne, thanks to this suffering – our comradeship, our loyalty, our humility, our courage, our generosity, the greatness of heart which has grown out of all this and when they come to judgement, let all the fruits which we have borne be their forgiveness.

Such a flowering of love amid the mess of life is surely a gift of the Spirit. It bears that peace which the world cannot give (John 14.27). But the question remains: how can I describe the interaction between the Spirit of God and my intellect in all of this?

Much of human awareness and personality – both its good and bad traits – depends on the way in which our brains function. Abnormality or accidental damage to our brains can result in dramatic changes in a person's behaviour. The now well-known story of Phineas Gage is a warning against any false dualism we might assume or invent to define the difference between mind, body and spirit. Gage, a much respected foreman supervising the laying of railway track in the United States in 1848, was accidentally injured when an iron rod entered his skull. He appeared to escape serious injury and returned to work soon afterwards. However, it was soon discovered that, as a result of the iron bar damaging his orbitofrontal cortex, he changed from being a pleasant and conscientious worker prior to the accident to being someone who was constantly rude, disrespectful and uncollaborative.

An individual's outlook and personality are subject to the same laws of creative process as the rest of creation, where lures compete with one another for life and death. So we need to be particularly prayerfully reflective when brain malfunction or damage appears to lock someone into a room we ourselves cannot enter, as in dementia for example. For it would be easy to conclude that mind and spirit are one and the same, which, of course, they are not. The spirit may well be observed through the personality but while Holy and human spirits affect and find expression through personality, they are not defined by it.

A principal part of authentic prayer is to do with that process of internal becoming where, at the highest and lowest levels of spiritual and mental awareness, the Holy Spirit can transform our minds and then our hearts by the power and presence of creative love. St Paul expressed this when he said, 'Do not be conformed to this world, but be transformed by the renewing of your minds, so that you may discern what is the will of God – what is good and acceptable and perfect' (Rom. 12.2). Then and only then can we learn to look at the world and ourselves through God's eyes, namely the eyes of the heart, as our prayer descends from the mind to the heart.

> I find Thee enthroned in my heart,
> my Lord Jesus.
> It is enough.
> I know that Thou art throned
> in heaven.
> My heart and heaven are one.[37]

St Paul also writes: 'God, who searches the heart, knows what is the mind of the Spirit, because the Spirit intercedes for the saints according to the will of God' (Rom. 8.27). To the extent that I have decided to surrender myself to this prayer, I have given in to the action of God both within and upon my heart.

This is a kind of kenosis, a process of self-emptying. I have accepted that my life is incomplete and unfulfilled without God and I have begun to get rid of all that is not 'of God' in me. But giving in like this means that rather than being diminished by prayer, I discover by prayer at the heart of myself who I am.

The unceasing prayer of God in my heart is balanced by the knowledge that the context of my life has changed. Having been created with free will I retain the ability to decide whether to promote or destroy life. But the way in which my mind has been renewed means not only that I am increasingly likely to make decisions that promote life over death, but also that, regardless of what may happen to me in the future, my heart is at one with the heart of creation.

So by the grace of God and within the love of the Divine Trinity – creation, salvation and redemption – I have forged my own salvation, and my faith, at long last, has been the catalyst for my growing up rather than the cause of constant immaturity.

4

Emerging love

Humility

As I have begun to believe in myself again, my faith in life – in God – has changed considerably. The two now seem inextricably entwined. While I have no wish to deny his ultimate power, my understanding of God as authoritarian ruler has died. Now I understand him primarily in terms of love.

I did wonder for a while whether I was simply reinventing God for my own purposes. However, I do not feel this is what I am doing. For God has been hard to get hold of. He emerges from the shadows only a bit at a time. If I were using the idea of him to legitimize my own agenda, I am sure I could have found a more straightforward way to do it.

It is very hard to hold on to your individuality when you inherit a faith which seems to have been owned by others for over two thousand years. Christianity, of course, has its roots in the monotheism of the Jewish religion so this adds about another two thousand years. I sometimes think it must have been much easier to have been a Christian in the first century. There would have been less theology and history to learn and assimilate. So I am not surprised when sometimes I feel suffocated by the theology of some of my ancestors, which has arisen out of a very different culture from my own.

I have now decided to decline the offer of a faith that cannot make sense of my life. This involves me in a reinterpretation of the truth rather than its rejection. As a consequence, my faith is much more honest. It now allows me to relate to myself without fear or guilt. Yet it does not deny my light or my darkness. It takes the whole of me and relates me to the wholeness of God.

Rather than arising out of my imagination, my knowledge and experience of God have arisen out of a continuous, developing dialogue between my humanity and my surroundings. I am driven from within by the creative Spirit who urges me on and on. Here I sense God in the yearning of the human spirit to reach beyond the mundane, to see beyond the stars, and to reach the goal of that search where God speaks to God.

Of those who saw it, who can forget the awful sight of the space shuttle Challenger exploding soon after take-off on 28 January 1986? All the members of the crew lost their lives. I remember Senator John Glenn – the first American to orbit the earth – reflecting on these events, saying, 'There is triumph and tragedy in the field of human endeavour.' And the dividing line between triumph and tragedy is thinner than we often realize. This reminds me that in both small and great, unrecognized and highly publicized undertakings, there is always a risk, especially when the ambitions of human beings come into play. Our best attempts to triumph can end up in tragedy. Sometimes, perhaps invariably, we have to encounter the tragedy before we can find the triumph.

The tragedy of the Challenger shuttle is a symbol both of the creativity of the human spirit and its moments of disastrous failure. It also reminds me that at the heart of the mission of Creative Love – at every step along the way – there stands a cross.

On the Challenger spacecraft an avoidable failure in the fuel supply suddenly changed a dramatic ascent towards earth orbit into a sickening and tragic descent into the Pacific Ocean. Here for all to see was a vivid reminder that every major quest on which we embark can be balanced on a hair's breadth. Rarely can we predict with certainty which way anything will go.

This knife edge between success and failure, survival and death, applies to the world of spiritual development, too. Moreover, it seems that many of the laws that apply to physical evolution apply also to the spiritual journey.

The recorded history of the spiritual development of humanity is testimony to this. Countless generations and close to one hundred thousand religions over the years reveal the spiritual evolution that is latent in creation yet visible in human beings. There are different expressions of spirituality among different kinds of people, and our understanding of these things seems to grow and develop with each generation.

Within this process, the Spirit of God can make itself known in the eloquence of a godly human life. At another time it can be stifled by the horrifying screams of human abuse and fearful obedience to a loveless god.

There are echoes of this spiritual development in my own personal spiritual growth. My development has taken me from the rigid structures of tribal religion to the more fluid spirituality of Divine Love. I have moved from spiritual immaturity, superstition, unmoving theism and legalism to something much more authentic and deeply involved in my everyday experience.

At long last I feel as if I 'own' my faith. And I cannot begin to express adequately the sense of freedom this brings. This is in stark contrast to how it was before. Then so much was handed down to me. 'Received wisdom' was delivered with the morning milk, if you like, and I accepted it because of my over-respectful attitude towards tradition.

Please don't misunderstand. I have no ambition to 'own' God. To 'download' him to the extent that he only moves at my command. But I sense that as I come to see more of God in and around me, I am becoming somehow incorporated into his being. Sometimes this feeling is so strong that I want to say 'I am a part of God'.

I suspect many will know what I mean. But to the ears of some who have bought into traditional, delivered religion this probably sounds blasphemous. I suppose that if I were to choose something from the vocabulary of the New Testament, I would say that after all these years of looking outside, I have now discovered 'Christ within myself' (Gal. 2.20). So perhaps this is not blasphemous after all. Maybe the blasphemy belongs with those who spurn spiritual freedom for a fake religious fear of a God who won't let them be themselves.

My deeper contemplation has made me exchange my old religious ways for a new Christian spirituality. Well, new to me, anyway. I seem to remember that Archbishop William Temple said, 'Remember that Christianity is not, first and foremost, a religion; it is first and foremost a revelation.'[1] He realized that religious structures can perpetuate false dualisms between God and godlessness, sacred and secular, spiritual and physical. Above all, while seeking to promote it, they can inhibit the individual's relationship with God.

Returning to my contemplation of the nature of the life in a garden, I can see an interrelatedness in creation that the Church by and large today struggles to recognize. Furthermore, as soon as we lose sight of the Spirit of life in all things, our church buildings and our Sunday gatherings only serve to emphasize the false dualisms that so often separate us from the Spirit of God in creation.

So where do we go from here? Where do we find hope?

Maybe the only future the Church has is in the abandonment of itself to the creative Spirit of the universe. Didn't Jesus say, 'those who want to save their life will lose it, and those who lose their life for my sake, and for the sake of the gospel, will save it' (Mark 8.35)?

Perhaps I should be spending my time discussing with the people I seek to serve how best to re-engage religion with the Spirit of love that exists at all levels of life. For when we live within the life of the Spirit – this energy of God that holds everything together in creative purpose – we grow up much more quickly.

As I develop these thoughts, I feel that I am moving on from the language and style of myth to that of mystery.

Implicit in the myth is the truth that while God is ultimately in control, he works through creation according to the processes of his love and in the context of the Fall as interpreted in a pre-universal setting. The mystery is more to do with how we try and make sense of the life that follows on from this. More importantly, it should help us to understand that when we fall – as inevitably we will – we need not only to pick ourselves up but also to try our best not to fall over in quite the same way again.

In many ways, we have a more developed way of understanding the life, death and resurrection of Jesus Christ than did the first Apostles if only because we have the benefit of historical perspective. I am not suggesting that previous 'editions' of the myth are somehow inaccurate or wrong or that we should change the myth itself. I believe that that revelation was and is very good. But while the myth is sacred, its mystery should be expressed by using the tools at the disposal of each generation. And no one human being, even the most enlightened, knows it all. Origen – whose theological insights we found so helpful earlier on – believed the spirit of humanity was incarcerated in a physical body from which it needed purification and ultimately escape. Today we think differently not least because of our advanced scientific knowledge, and to this we shall return.

We have to avoid the spiritual neurosis that religion provokes when it refuses to reinterpret the images of the past. It is not possible nor is it desirable for human beings in the twenty-first century to try and believe and behave in the same way as human beings did in the first century. While the first followers of Christ believed in a three-tier universe, we do not. They believed that epilepsy was caused by demons. We do not. This need not, however, make our understanding of evil any the less real. Nor does it mean that we have to go soft on the forces of evil that can wreak havoc on human relationships.

The teaching of Jesus was radical and revolutionary. He sat light to tradition wherever the traditions of the ancestors or of the religious leaders overlooked, ignored or actively worked against the purposes of authentic love. The love of Christ was inclusive not exclusive. He did not teach that the people of God consisted only of those who were tied to one particular nation's interpretation of the truth. Jesus taught that God was bigger than any one tradition. And he said that this was a God that was to be found not by some kind of neurotic search for religious purity but through what you were prepared to surrender and give away in the often untidy and unpredictable ways of sacrificial love.

The condemnation that the cross can bring about, therefore, is not for those who fail to live up to impossible moral standards or those who fail to keep up their subscription to their local or national church institution. It is for those who prevent others from being themselves, for those who make us feel guilty for being ourselves and for those who try to define truth for the sake of their own self-preservation.

Religious structures promise great security, while the kind of self-abandonment I am speaking about is scary stuff. Self-abandonment stands in direct contrast to the way we are biologically programmed and socially conditioned today to hold on to whatever we can, rather than let go. The function of the gospel is to confront and challenge the desire to acquire and accumulate with a love whose freedom is found in the process of letting go. For when we turn our backs on the acquisition of power, we discover that human relationships can be based on mutual love rather than materialism.

One of the principal ways of 'letting go' within the processes of creation is the practice of humility. Another scary concept. The trouble is that humility has for many become synonymous with weakness. In a capitalist society that is driven by the evolutionary perspective of the survival of the fittest this, too, runs contrary to many modern criteria of success.

To be humble really means to live in the knowledge that we are of the earth (*humus*, meaning 'ground'). The author of the second chapter of Genesis, writing in Hebrew, says that *adam* (human being) was formed from *adamah* (the dust of the ground or earth, Gen. 2.7). But we have agreed that we are not mere earth. For this is dust into which God has breathed – and continues to breathe – his life. This is the Divine exhalation that fills the universe following the Big Bang to which we referred earlier. We are carbon-based life forms and the carbon in our bodies that originated in the heart of a star guides us to find the Christ of the universe within the humble earthly dwelling of ourselves.

Humility is not about self-negation. For this kind of lack of self-confidence denies the image of God in us. To interpret humility simply in terms of being everyone's doormat sells short the servanthood we are called to offer. I do not see any trace of that kind of desecration of divinity in the life of Christ.

Humility was once described by Simone Weil as 'the refusal to exist outside God'.[2] For me this is grounded in the need to contemplate – or see – our lives in the context of a constant dialogue or prayer with the God who is all and in all (1 Cor. 15.28; Eph. 1.23). In addition to the rational decisions we might make as we move step by step towards God, we discover a spiritual reorientation that happens quite imperceptibly by grace. As Julian of Norwich reminds us, 'God's will is that by faith we should see him continually, though it seems to us that we are seeing him so little.'[3]

So having rescued myself from the altar of ecclesiastical conformity, where now should I look to see this deeply identifying and self-emptying (kenotic) God at work?

God's creative energy

The simple answer to this question has to be 'everywhere'. According to William Blake, 'Everything that lives is Holy.'[4] But within this 'everywhere' and 'everything' I see God in particular – in the life of creation since the pre-universal Fall – as the Divine energy that produces order and life from disorder and death in ever-increasing degrees of complexity.

I can best describe this as the 'lure for order' in what we call the lower forms of life and the 'lure to love' in the higher forms.

My understanding of the Christian story helps me to recognize an unmistakable creative drive within an evolving world that labours ceaselessly so that 'things will turn out right'. As Diarmuid O'Murchu points out:

> The sense of purpose is all pervasive and deeply ingrained in the fabric of the universe. Even the curvature of space itself is delicately poised – between the demise of collapse into a massive black hole, had the initial curvature been a fraction larger, or an explosion into a scattering of lifeless particles, had it been a fraction smaller . . . Only when we realise that we humans are totally dependent on the material of the stars (carbon) for our existence, and that the very creation of that substance is something of a cosmic miracle, can we begin to contemplate *purpose*, not in terms of final outcome, but in the very process and nature of evolution itself.[5]

There are those who reduce the creative advance of life simply to the need of genes to survive and replicate. By constructing complex machines for themselves, genes ensure the continued existence of human beings. So some biologists might describe God as the 'origin of ultimate units of matter' but not as the creator of the species.[6] For them the real driving forces of evolution are natural selection and mutation.

I don't find this a satisfactory argument at all. I still have to ask why I can detect a forward or developing momentum to creation. There is chaos, sure. But there is order, too. And the way I see it – despite the chaos with which we are confronted daily – order is winning. Maybe only just, but winning it is.

We can observe this 'lure' that things should turn out right in the way the DNA in our bodies is distributed to each cell, which itself has a complete copy of all the DNA properties in our bodies. Why should DNA molecules grow in complexity from one cell at conception to approximately one thousand million million at adulthood? While mistakes occur from time to time, the unconscious molecules are nonetheless programmed to produce further life rather than death and distinction. Why? In anthropomorphic terms, why do they want to survive? Or, to put it another way, why is the biology of life stronger than the biology of death?

Given this inner momentum towards life, we reasonably expect cells to divide in ways that promote individual and corporate health and wholeness. So we feel deeply the pain caused when this doesn't happen.

Understandably, we cry out against nature when life 'turns out wrong' because we know that the momentum of the world's energies is geared heavily so that life should 'turn out right'. Let us take, for example, cells that are discovered to have divided in such a way as to cause cancer.

> Cells make this mistake fairly regularly, but the body has elaborate mechanisms for dealing with it. It is only very rarely that the process spirals out of control. On average, humans suffer one fatal malignancy for each 100 million billion cell divisions.[7]

Or to put it another way, God's way with the world has always been about its redemption. There are myriad 'decisions' being made all the time throughout creation between further and more developed possibilities of life and that distortion of creative energy that leads to death. This in Christian terms is what we might call the difference between the transfiguration and disfiguration of creation. The cancerous cells that inhabit a child's body are not the result of the sins of his or her parents or grandparents. That kind of religious answer is nonsense today. Instead we may say that these cells are present because the Divine energy in creation has been confused, obstructed, diverted, negated. Here, again, we see how spiritual fallout has contaminated our world.

It is in this lure to life amid the decisions for death that we find the Spirit of God in intimate and unconditional relationship with all the processes of life that make up this world. For the Divine energy that moved over the face of the waters at the beginning of time is the same energy that is at the heart of God. He is the reason why there is any life at all as we know it.

This energy which we identify as creative love – the very energy or love of God – can alone bring about the redemption of humanity, the cosmos and indeed the universe (Rom. 8.11):

> It is the Life-Giver who enables the movement of the unfolding of the early universe from the Big Bang, the beginning of nuclear processes in stars, the formation of our planetary system, the emergence of life on earth, and the evolution of self-conscious human beings. It is this same Spirit who empowers the life and ministry of Jesus of Nazareth within our evolutionary and cultural history as the radically Spirit-filled human being.[8]

This is why there is such a central emphasis in the New Testament on the physical resurrection of Christ. By authentic love God has the power to redeem the world that is made of spirit fused with matter.

As a result, I prefer to think of the Christian life primarily as the way by which we can live in increasing harmony with the creative Spirit of God. This is far more important a starting point than an overbearing emphasis on the structures and systems of institutional life or personal morality as defined by a particular culture as an end in itself.

This developing convergence with the creative Spirit is the only possible future for Christianity. For the world has now seen through that kind of religion described by Philip Larkin as

that vast moth-eaten musical brocade
created to pretend we never die.[9]

All matter, of course, is comprised of energy. What we often regard as solid, inert and physical reality is better understood in terms of creative energy. What we refer to as physical objects are made up of attractions and reactions of molecular energy. And all the millions and millions of atoms involved – whose electrons are in perpetual motion – retain their particular identity. The same sub-atomic building blocks arranged differently produce both myself and the table upon which I am resting in order to write this.

We now understand that reality – often thought in the past to be comprised of fixed, unchanging physical properties – is made up of myriad relationships that are constantly on the move. For example, once two electrons 'have interacted with each other, they possess a power to influence each other however widely they subsequently separate', even if they are on opposite sides of the world.[10] And while there are some areas of creation that appear to behave in a set and predictable manner, 'most systems are so exquisitively sensitive to circumstance that the slightest disturbance will make them behave in a totally different way'.[11] We are all familiar with the way the weather in the United Kingdom can be affected by a butterfly flapping its wings on some far continent.

At various times mainstream Christians have often preferred to think of human beings as primarily defined by fixed points of reference. Our predilection for imposing a user-friendly order on the world to help us order our own relationships has meant that our religion has been a useful tool for spiritual conservationists. They have made the establishment of fixed points of so-called ultimate truth of prime importance. We should not forget, though, that formal religion has flourished for only 5 per cent of the time of human evolution.[12]

However, we now realize that reality is not about determinism but about relationships and their consequences. In realizing this we suddenly discover that the static Christ of so much formalized religion is released to become the free Spirit of the universe in human beings. And the life of this Spirit becomes fulfilled in the celebration of unrestricted love when things turn out right in the heart of the universe.

As we have seen, following the Big Bang, spirit and created matter were indefinably fused in the contaminated particles from which life eventually came. It is therefore a false distinction to separate matter from spirit within the human being.

'Reality' therefore is made up of energy that comes from God and is part of his being. Its 'forward' momentum – towards ever-greater complexity of life – is derived from his indwelling 'lure for life'. What is more, this creative energy or Spirit that has been producing order and harmony amid disorder and disharmony from the very beginning, is as a consequence able to 'feel' the failures and successes of the progress of the world. Whatever happens to or within the energy of the cosmos happens to God because, without being confined to it, he is the ground of its life.

It comes as no surprise to find that those who are deeply contemplative in a humble kind of way are more easily able to perceive the Divine in creation and therefore sense a oneness with the world.

Humility – being 'of the earth' in the sense that we are one with the creative energies of life – helps us to identify with St Francis of Assisi in his recognition of the sacramental nature of creation, most popularly remembered in his address to Brother Sun and Sister Moon.

We can no longer regard the trees that surround us as mere physical objects. We are 'interrelated' by the way we share the building blocks of creation. When I inadvertently return to relating to the world in terms of a subject–object relationship, I need only to remind myself that chlorophyll – the green colouring in the leaves of the trees by which they turn sunlight into energy – is only one carbon different from the blood without which I cannot live.

One of my most powerful experiences of this interrelatedness came one day when I had fallen asleep while sitting with my back against the trunk of a tree. I don't know how long I was there, but when I woke up I found that a spider had woven its web in such a way as to make me feel that I was blended into the tree. This was an occasion when mysticism became tangible for me. For a moment it seemed that I was physically, spiritually and visibly at one with nature and the processes of the Creator.

There is an eloquence in this picture that I cannot put into words. But what I can say is that false dualisms between physical and spiritual are now extinct. I have lost human objectivity in the subjectivity of the life of God.[13]

Let me repeat. Developing a spirit of humility is thought by some to be a kind of spiritual snobbery. Nothing could be further from the truth. For humility in essence recognizes our need to live daily and at depth with the God who constitutes our very nature.

Inevitably, therefore, humility also involves both affirmation and praise of the God who is everywhere. Surely this was what the Psalmist was referring to when he wrote: 'Where can I go from your spirit? Or where can I flee from your presence?' (Ps. 139.7). For this sort of humility is both awe-inspiring and frightening, exciting and intimidating in the immensity of creation and the boundlessness of God's love. Again the Psalmist says: 'When I look at your heavens, the work of your fingers, the moon and the stars that you have established; what are human beings that you are mindful of them, mortals that you care for them?' (Ps. 8.3–4).

As I hold on to and nurture this insight, I realize once again that a constant humble offering of myself like this means that my life itself is likely to become a prayer, in its constant – and maybe one day ceaseless – dialogue with God. There is no dipping in and dipping out of the presence of God; no God on just Sunday and on odd occasions during the week. There is only the life of God.

This is the seamless robe worn by Christ, for which at the foot of his cross those whose hearts were pagan and cold cast lots (John 19.23–24). They greedily tried to purchase for themselves what they took to be a magic mantle that would help them in their grasping endeavour for power and authority, material wealth and worldly security. Their sweaty palms, clenched tight in the obscenity of their self-interest, revealed their rejection of any kind of divine co-existence. This was in stark contrast to the open and bleeding hands of sacrificial love whose meaning was truly and absolutely over their heads.

There are several messages here for our Church and for our materialistic society. Not least is the warning that you cannot have what Christ offers by financial transaction any more than Christians themselves can put their faith or their Church up for sale (1 Cor. 9.18). Then there is the message that those who assume the Christian mantle to promote their own power and authority either with God or with the world or both are not simply mistaken but gambling with the life of God as heartless materialists. And there is the challenge that if you really want a share in the life of Christ, there is only one way to find it. And that is to live your life in such a way that immerses yourself in the love of God and the love of God in your self. This undivided, incorporated and seamless existence overcomes hellish nightmares of unfulfilled potential as earth and heaven become one in the unrestricted ascent of our soul into God. For this is a life lived with all its ups and downs, joys and sorrows, crucifixions and resurrections within the heart of God.

This is surely what we mean when we refer to the sacramental nature of the world. For the bread and wine that we call the body and blood of Christ on our holy tables are symbols of the ways in which God shares his life sacrificially with us and gathers up our life and that of the universe in his life. As a consequence of this perception and the prayer that it produces, the way in which I live and relate to the whole of creation changes dramatically.

I have now taken to bowing to everyone with whom I shake hands. I do this to acknowledge the God I see in them. This bowing of mine invariably elicits powerful reactions, especially among those who feel they have an ecclesiastical position that requires some kind of ex officio respect. 'Ha ha! There's no need to bow to me,' they say. 'Ha ha,' I reply, 'I'm not bowing to you but to the Christ who lives in you whom I serve.' By contrast, when I shake hands and bow to my Hindu and Sikh friends there is no such misunderstanding. They simply bow back. I bow to trees, animals, hills and rivers, too, but only when there is no one watching.

Please don't misunderstand. As I mentioned earlier, I am not suggesting that by identifying deeply with the world, God is somehow trapped within it. To believe that God is both incarnate within the world and also above and beyond it is central to our faith. It is foolish to try and restrict God to one place as if he were a human being or a force that can be contained or controlled. While God chose to be vulnerable in his creativity, there is no need to assume that at the same time he surrendered his individuality to it.

I realize this is a very anthropomorphic way of understanding God, but if this is a way we can begin to describe how authentic love operates in and through human beings, there is no reason why we should not surmise that the same kind of principles of love are found in God. I think we have already established that the source of creative love is far bigger than any one person or aspect of creation, or even any human description, can encompass.

Love in disorder

We may now see how the Spirit of creative love has emerged by various stages from Divine energy in the building blocks of creation to the Divine life of Jesus Christ in human beings. Not forgetting that all the way along this journey of developing identity, the Spirit has had to grow in and through a creation that is constantly affected by fallouts in relationships.

Nevertheless, we can observe that there is an undeniable 'lure for life' in the aggression by which an animal secures food for itself and its close relatives. But we can also see that this survival is likely to come at the expense of the life of another. My appreciation of the care a lioness gives to her cubs is balanced by my sadness at the terror she causes in a gazelle as she chases it close to exhaustion and savagely kills it.

We can also see how this 'lure for life' surfaces through aggressive behaviour among human beings in the hunting and killing of prey and in the way that tribes and nations space themselves out so that natural resources needed for survival are secured. Here again one group usually benefits at the expense of another where energy resources such as oil are concerned.

In the life of the individual, the progress of the inner 'lure for life' is advanced in many ways by the presence of pain. In fact, while you would not normally wish pain on someone else, evolution cannot do without it. For pain in animals and human beings warns the body of hunger, injury, thirst and the need to rest.

But we cannot speak about a 'lure for life' without also acknowledging a 'lure for death' which is the cause of much suffering in the lower and higher forms of life. In humanity, genetically determined behaviour that favours the survival of the fittest stands in stark contrast to a developing care and concern for the weak as well as the strong. While the ancient Spartans would risk the lives of their babies by leaving them on the side of a mountain for a night as a test of their hardiness for life ahead, we tend to try and move mountains to save the lives of babies born in difficult circumstances. At this level we speak not of competing 'lures' but of good versus evil, life versus death.

In this environment, creative love begins to emerge in human beings most noticeably in loving relationships and in the care of parents for their offspring. While the latter can be largely determined by genetic conditioning in animals, it finds greater expression in human beings. So the one is linked to the other: 'The possibility for the emergence of self-giving and self-sacrificing behaviour in nonhuman primates, as well as in lower organisms, may . . . be seen as part of the intrinsic pattern of creation.'[14] This is what I understand Christians to mean when they describe humanity as having been created in the image of God. As I have said, of all creation, it is only human beings who have the potential to love as God loves, that is, without conditions. This is what sets us apart from – but not above – the rest of creation.

What is more, it is important we realize that as the Holy Spirit has grown to express its true identity and fullness of being through evolutionary processes, it has emerged from being recognized as the 'lure for life' amid the contamination of spiritual fallout, to being seen as the creative energy that confronts evolutionary evil with the demands of the kingdom of love.

There are those, of course, who think that there is no such thing as pure altruism. They believe that so-called altruism and love exist only because of their species survival value. So altruism is really genetically inspired selfishness. This is as true in parenting as it can be in gifts of overseas aid to the developing world. People rarely give without expecting something in return. When they don't consciously expect something, they are nevertheless being driven by unconscious desires. Rather than being the result of holy living and God-centred lives, self-sacrifice and saintliness are understood by the reductionists as simply a part of our genetic make-up. They have similar views concerning religious systems that underwrite forms of social behaviour that have been found to be successful tools in the evolutionary struggle for survival.

It is undeniable that there is a great deal of selfish behaviour that passes as altruism and that systems of good faith have been consistently hijacked to provide cultural plausibility for greedy and devious political ends.[15] However, to describe human beings as mere gene-survival machines is in direct contrast to a belief that the whole of creation is filled by the breath or Spirit of God. It is difficult to argue against biological reductionism other than by making spiritual assertions as we come up against not even God made in the image of man, which we abhor, but even worse – God in the image of a gene.[16]

While possessing great knowledge of the design of the world, some see no place for a grand Designer. Life has evolved because the necessary physical properties required have existed and that's it. Looking for any kind of eternity or meaning beyond the mundane is fruitless as far as this rather fatalistic understanding of creation goes. But there can be no long-term future in a scheme where, instead of a Spirit of redemption giving direction and meaning to evolutionary advance, we assume god-like qualities by the ethics of consensus ourselves.

It is probable that some genes or clusters of genes may give a predisposition to the development of religious orientation, or at least generate a brain that is more sensitive than usual to the emotions and feelings of other people. But they cannot themselves invent revelation or redemption. Nor do we need to regard the gene and species-preserving functions of formal religion as being the only reason for its existence.

It is surely reasonable to say that the spiritual 'lure for life' could produce a gene that enhances the spiritual and religious development of the individual and group. On the other hand, it may be that so-called clusters of religious genes 'absorb' revelation as a life-enhancing component for their protection and that of the species.

I find it far more exciting and enriching to understand genetic research as the latest and one of the most powerful ways in which we can co-operate with God in the ongoing life of creation.

In a world where nothing enters ready-made we – more than any previous generation – can take great steps to free the Spirit of creative love from its contaminated environment. The identification of genes that give a predisposition to cancer and Alzheimer's disease, for example, and responsible stem-cell research provide us with great opportunities to enhance the possibilities for life at the expense of the possibilities for suffering and death. When we act in this way, we fulfil the purpose and processes of creation with God, as we promote the triumph of love over the tragedy of pain.

This, surely, is part and parcel of what it means to pray that God's kingdom comes when his will is done on earth as it is in heaven. To embark on genetic research and development away from the context of Divine creation is frightening. As I said earlier, left to its own devices, humanity can make decisions in the cause of self-interest that can have horrifying results.

On the other hand, when Divine love emerges through the reflective awareness of the human species or the level of consciousness we have reached, there is always hope of redemption.[17] It is here more than anywhere else that we can observe the emergence of God's Spirit of creative love.

An example of this comes from a remarkable episode in the history of the Maori tribes of New Zealand.[18] In the days of pre-European influence, the Maori were naturally aggressive towards one another. Hostilities between the 40 tribes were frequent. The result of this was the spacing out and stabilization of the population.

This stability was lost, however, when European firearms were acquired and used with devastating effect by those tribesmen who had them, against those who did not. There followed an arms race that was enormously costly in terms of lives lost. After twenty years of armed conflict, one of the tribes without any external religious influence began seriously to question the point of fighting for revenge. As a result, what until then had been accepted methods of thought and action were abandoned. In the 1830s and 1840s the Maori as a whole converted to Christianity and warfare among the tribes ceased altogether.

But what was it that made them stop fighting? Was it some deep-seated biological mechanism within them that was to do with the survival of the species? Or was it a realization of the extent and meaninglessness of the carnage that so offended them? (A quarter of the total population died.)

We could say in some kind of self-righteous way that the Maori stopped fighting as a result of the success of missionary Christianity. This would be a perfectly plausible explanation. But why just then, at that particular moment, were the Maori ready to convert? There was a lot more going on than Christian evangelism. For prior to this conversion, the Maori were already developing a 'new perspective' on human relationships and the worth of the individual. Christian missionaries were then able to make the most of this fertile ground of new faith in humanity.

It is very unlikely that the change in attitude and the new perspective were due solely to genetic programming to protect the species or tribe as the fighting had only lasted twenty years. While in certain circumstances, such as major trauma, there may well be a fairly immediate impact on the genes with short-term consequences, it is unlikely that they will have adapted to this particular arms race that quickly. Genetic safeguards such as the introduction of appeasement gestures were not able to keep up with the proliferation of weapons of clinical destruction throughout the twentieth century, so it is unlikely that such genetic restraints could have been produced in a much shorter period of time. What we have here, then, is a negotiated peace that has not come about as a result of appeasement gestures but by a rational recognition of the senselessness of killing even if in the past it had produced the stabilizing and the spacing out of the population.

It is very likely that what we have here is an example of how the Spirit of creation was directly at work in the level of conscious awareness in the Maori people. Even if it had its origins in their genetic make-up, we can still argue that it was because of their spiritual awakening that the Maori (in this instance) were able to recognize the futility and meaninglessness of their aggression. This more than anything else may well have prepared them to accept the Christian gospel.

This process will have been repeated countless times all over the world at different stages in the spiritual evolution of humanity. And it is ongoing not least as we face the threat posed by weapons of mass destruction.

Let me give just one other example of how the emergence of the Spirit of creative love through the processes of evolution has influenced the development of human behaviour, leading us from slavish obedience to base instincts to unconditional loving. This can be seen in the way the brain has developed.

Generally speaking, the brain has developed in three phases.[19] The hindbrain and midbrain came first, and these structures mediate survival instincts. The forebrain is more recent and is the part that has evolved the most. The forebrain itself contains many structures, most significantly the 'middle-aged' structures of the limbic system and the vast cerebral cortex which is the 'newest' part. The cortex is especially large and evolved in the human brain. It is responsible for processing sensory information to a very high degree so that we have a detailed consciousness of the world about us, together with flexible decision-making processes based on reason, emotion and memory. These give us a level of voluntary control over our behaviour far beyond that of even our closest relatives, the primates.

The middle-aged limbic system includes a pair of structures known as the amygdala. These structures are central to emotional functions and act as go-betweens, taking in highly processed information from the cortex – more developed in human beings than in any other species – which is telling them what is happening 'out there' and organizing an appropriate emotional response by calling on the older structure of the mid- and hindbrain. So, for example, in response to an external threat, the amygdala will send commands to the midbrain so that the cortex can think fast and release adrenaline into the bloodstream which puts the brain and body into 'high-performance' mode.

The amygdala is older in evolutionary terms than the cortex and while in human beings it is larger and more developed, it has greater similarity to the amygdala of other animals than the cerebral cortex. The fact that human emotional behaviour is so varied and flexible is explained primarily not only in terms of the enlargement of the amygdala, but also by the fact that it is working with a uniquely powerful and advanced cortex. So while the amygdala of other mammals receives and responds to information in an inflexible and instinctive manner (these mammals feel hungry, smell food and attack), our amygdala can be so regulated by the cortex, where more developed options than the instinctual are housed, that our behaviour is more socially aware and civilized (we may feel hungry, smell food but, because it belongs to someone else, refrain from eating it).

However, sometimes when circumstances push us too hard, if we are starving or our lives are being threatened, the amygdala can overpower the cortex and produce a more innate, instinctive reaction. So without thinking, we take what food is available to us even if this means someone else near us will die as a result.

The way in which the human brain has evolved reveals how the Spirit of God has emerged increasingly in the evolution of human beings and we are beckoned to replace instinctive behaviour with unconditional love. The renewing of the human mind consists of having to fight constantly against our natural inclinations especially when we are feeling threatened. For human becoming to take place, the evolutionary drives of the survival of the fittest have to give way to the inspiration of the Spirit that promotes the kingdom of God. Here self-preservation at the expense of others gives way to sacrificial love. It is in this context that Christ commands us to love our enemies, render no one evil for evil and to pray for those who persecute us (Matt. 5.21–48).

This kingdom is central to the teaching of Jesus. In contrast to the kingdoms of this world, this kingdom is to be found in the heart of the believer where the Spirit of Christ transforms our inner selves from self-centredness to self-offering. This rule and reign of God in our hearts brings about not only a transformation of ourselves but also of society and is fundamental to God's work of redemption. This is why Jesus says that above all else, we should first seek the kingdom of God (Matt. 6.33; Luke 12.31) and that we should seek and find this foremost within ourselves (Luke 17.21). The kingdom of God is also referred to as the kingdom of heaven, reminding us that redemption consists of restoring the relationship between earth and heaven, creation with its Creator, as we fall out with one another less and less and learn instead how to fall in love, completely and utterly.

Our understanding of how the brain works also confirms our holistic approach to human being. Just as the ancient Hebrew belief was that body and spirit are one, so, for different reasons to do with our scientific understanding of brain functions, we can no longer think of the mind as spirit and the body as matter.

While the spirit of who we are can be described as eternal in the sense that it is part of the Spirit of creation, our minds are not independent of our bodies. Our minds and personalities are instead dependent upon the activities of our brains. Our sense of self, our developing free will and decision-making all depend upon the pre-frontal networks of our brains functioning in harmony. Whereas reason and emotion used to be seen as belonging to different sides of our brains, it is now becoming clear that intelligent, reasonable, adaptive behaviour is not reason without emotion but rather reason and emotion in balance.

In fact, we may say that 'there seem to be common subconscious mechanisms of our species in response to moral challenges . . . Somehow it would seem that the universally recognized mechanisms of self-survival have been co-opted and are used to work in more social settings.'[20]

Wherever people of good faith come together – and this will inevitably involve those from different cultures and religions – opportunities for re-creation and redemption arise. Our search for peace therefore is likely to be fruitless until we permit the power of creative love within us to bring about a new perspective of forgiveness and healing.

So creative love surfaces in the spiritual life of humanity. By nature it is revolutionary rather than evolutionary. Love is not another piece of evolutionary equipment. While it works through evolution, it stands against the bias towards the survival of the fittest.

The purpose of love is to confront and overcome evil so that evil loses its power to produce pain in an indiscriminate and destructive manner. At the heart of the cosmos there is a cross that confronts evolutionary development wherever it is cruel rather than constructive. God stands as victim alongside all victims of aggression, calling the perpetrator to discover a better way, the way of unconditional love. From this cross he calls people of all backgrounds, nations and religions to work together for peace and justice.

The gift of contemplative prayer is part of the mystic's ability to see patterns of the Divine within creation, together with the meaning they convey. Mystics seem to see God particularly in that place where human and Holy Spirit coincide, retaining their vision even when there is an apparent absence of light. For emerging love in human consciousness generates an awareness that 'there is more to life than meets the eye'. The level of my reflective awareness – due to the development of my brain – gives me an insight into how life really is in a way that my dog lying at my feet cannot appreciate. I begin to recognize the cosmic Christ in the life of creation and in myself. Here my life finds meaning and purpose beyond genetics and neuroscience. So much so that I can begin to learn how to pray in a way that takes me beyond the physical to a deeper spiritual reality where I can reach out and, as it were, touch the Spirit of the living Christ.

Returning to the trees, I notice that while they have a beauty in the summer when the leaves are green, they look their best in the autumn when their leaves are dying. It is then that they display the most vivid and striking colour. And it is strange to think that my life has become most full of meaning on those occasions when I seem to have died to myself so completely. For while 'God did not make death, and he does not delight in the death of the living' (Wisd. 1.13), it is often when we come across the crucifixion of life that we realize that here he holds the power to reveal more about his transforming love than anywhere else. And as we have seen, in the process of dying to self almost on a daily basis, we find the way to love, freely and without fear.

As the Spirit of creative love achieves a greater level of self-expression in the possibilities that human beings have to love without conditions, we now understand that this refers not only to our relationships with one another but also with creation and especially with God.

To reach a sense of unconditional love for God is to experience an immense sense of freedom. While we like to speak of and celebrate the transforming love of God in Jesus Christ, we are usually reluctant or unable to love him in a similar fashion. We tend to put all sorts of conditions on our love of God. When they are not met, our faith tends to fail to some degree. But when we get away from constantly trying to get God to prove his love for us, when we love him for the joy of that love alone, we can rid ourselves of all the 'ifs, buts and maybes' of a faith that cannot see what Jesus means for us and for creation.

In loving God unconditionally we also find that the joy of the sacramental nature of the present moment is released and unrestricted. So what if we cannot prove all that we would like to about our faith. So what if God seems irresponsible, forgetful, uninterested, deaf and even malevolent at times. Unconditional love is focused purely on the Beloved.

So instead of concentrating first on trying to love others as Jesus Christ loves me, I concentrate instead on loving God as he loves me. Consequently, I am far more likely to love others in a similar fashion because at least I have learned how to live like this with God.

Now the more annoying habits of others, their irresponsibility, forgetfulness, lack of interest, deafness and even malevolence are far less likely to bother me and become a barrier to our relationships. For when in the self-awareness of human beings, the Spirit emerges as a stranger in an often hostile evolutionary process, it can release us to find the positive energy in all relationships. Here the Spirit creates not only a deeper appreciation of where the energy of love lies in creation but also an understanding of how best we can promote and celebrate it.

To learn how to love like this is the aim of the process whereby human beings become increasingly self-aware and open to the life-enhancing and redemptive possibilities of creative love.

We should never underestimate, though, how much we have to struggle to do this among and despite other competing agendas – our own and those of others – that will thwart our attempts to express our true identity. Central to the process of growing up is the need to grow away from any influences that inhibit our ability to be ourselves. These may include not only what we regard as bad but also good and even loving influences which have helped us for a while but from which we now need to move on.

While redemptive relationships are not confined to Christianity – the Divine Spirit belongs not to the Church but to creation – the Church should be heavily involved in promoting new kingdom relationships rather than old religion. As John Bowker reminds us:

> The opportunities of religion, to create the greatest good news and beauty in mind and spirit and behaviour, to find God by being found by God, to grasp the nettle and to grasp one's neighbour as being not other than oneself, none of this has disappeared. What has disappeared is the necessity for religions to guard and protect the process of gene replication. And the more a religion identifies itself with that necessity and refuses to relinquish it, the more absurd it becomes.[21]

One of the most moving descriptions concerning the fulfilment of the kingdom is to be found in the Old Testament and written by the prophet Isaiah.

> The wolf shall live with the lamb,
>   the leopard shall lie down with the kid,
> the calf and the lion and the fatling together,
>   and a little child shall lead them.

The cow and bear shall graze,
their young shall lie down together;
and the lion shall eat straw like the ox.
The nursing child shall play over the hole of the asp,
and the weaned child shall put its hand on the adder's den.
They will not hurt or destroy
on all my holy mountain;
for the earth will be full of the knowledge of the LORD
as the waters cover the sea.

(Isa. 11.6–9)

For many the significance of this passage is that it is an image of how life will be when creation is fulfilled and the kingdom of God is established. In the temporal sense this will take place at the end-time when God finally acts to bring earth and heaven together.

But we can also recognize here words that are meant to transform our understanding of the present. The author wants us to know that when we are confronted by the beastliness of nature, particularly when it causes the death of those humans considered most innocent and vulnerable, there is always hope. For as many times as our experience of life leads us towards a godless despair, we can be comforted by the knowledge that this is not how it will be for ever. In particular, we know that our suffering now is neither random nor meaningless.

Faith falling into place

As a result of this approach, I can move on from my anger, misgivings and misunderstanding of the miraculous power of God and see it now in a new light.

I can see that I was wrong to think of miracles predominantly in terms of justice. My thinking was purely conditional. God needs to perform miracles in order to establish justice in an unjust world, I said. Or, the absence of miracles indicates that God is unconcerned with matters of justice. Or, miracles cannot exist without some explicit or implicit statement about justice.

This misunderstanding came from a strong desire to see an end to unjust suffering. I also realize that there is a subconscious consumerism here that expects God to respond to my faith in the way I feel is right.

But the ways of logic and love do not always lead in the same direction. Justice would have seen Judas crucified, not Jesus. Logic fails to comprehend the cross. As Mother Julian says, for our good alone Christ would have suffered more if it had been possible,[22] which is a senseless statement in the eyes of cold logic.

In the Fourth Gospel miracles are 'signs' of God's love and indicators of his eternal life. They are not God's conjuring tricks to encourage faith by sleight of hand. Lazarus is raised from the dead by the one who through himself can grant resurrection and life. Lazarus, however, eventually dies because he is mortal. The five thousand who were once miraculously fed on a hillside would have become hungry again. Instead, these events are signs of the new order breaking into the present. They point away from ourselves and to the life God wants us all to enjoy. It is a life in which we are all invited to share, both now and in eternity.

I understand also that a sign is granted sometimes to an individual as part of the unfolding of the grace of God in his or her life. This is usually to prepare or equip them for new work in the kingdom. We have already talked about how the risen Christ met Saul on the road to Damascus as an occasion to be understood as a sign of something that lies ahead rather than some kind of spiritual stunt.

More significant, however, given what we now know about the processes of love, are those miracles that come about when the love of God in creation comes to the surface in forgiving love – as opposed to 'reaching in from outside' – in often apparently godless circumstances.

Common to all these types of miracle is the way they are associated with the emergence of love through suffering. It is not usual for them to be about the complete and permanent relief of suffering. Usually they occur in order that we may continue to bear suffering. Invariably they produce in us a quality of authentic love that we can acquire in no other way. The prayer found in Ravensbruck concentration camp to which I referred on page 91 is a good example of this.

Having liberated my understanding of miracles from the context of justice, I do not wish to suggest that I do not believe that God is not passionately concerned with such issues. A denial of justice for human beings always involves a denial of God's image in them. However, God's justice is not won by force but by love. Not by a change of law but by a change of heart. Religious people often think mistakenly that justice comes by power and often through military intervention. Instead, it is realized in the untidy, demanding and frequently painful ways of love.

I realize now that it was a mark of my spiritual immaturity to expect God to perform miracles like a doctor who possesses a cure-all tonic. After all, Jesus himself wasn't able to heal everyone, if only because he couldn't get to them all. (This simple fact makes me even more wary of those who claim that the only reason Jesus doesn't heal is down to our doubts and guilt.)

In the past when a miracle occurred in my own life I could never accept it as such. This is not because I lacked faith or because I didn't spend sufficient time in earnest prayer. I was unable to recognize the activity of the Spirit in such an event because my eyes had become focused somewhere other than upon God. I had decided that justice and the dealings of an interventionist deity were the only context for the interpretation of miracles. I was focusing all my attention on gaining exemption from suffering. I did this at the expense of concentrating my energy on being with God, uniting my will with his. To put it another way, I had forgotten the need to try and assimilate my feeble attempts at love into the processes of his authentic love.

Now, despite my occasional cries for help, my desire for miracles has all but gone. It now pales into insignificance in comparison with my desire to live ever closer to Christ. After all, didn't he say it was an adulterous and evil generation that looked for miracles beyond the resurrection (Matt. 12.39; 16.4; Mark 8.12; Luke 11.29)?

My greatest intention now is to look out constantly for God. I know that if I can do this, my life will inevitably be changed. This will take place not by my fevered discipleship but by the mystery of Divine love acting on my spirit.

As I grow up, I can now stop behaving like a spoilt child always asking favours of an indulgent parent. My prayers of petition and intercession are no longer dominated by selfish desires for greater comfort and safety. For too long I have been like a child playing in his bedroom periodically calling out to God to fix me some tea, mend the toys I have broken or find the ones I have lost.

The biggest miracle of life is found in death. By this I mean that as my prayer life develops, death ceases to describe only the termination of my life. For I now understand death in terms of various qualities of life.

As my prayerful contemplation of my own existence deepens, death loses its power to destroy me or my loves or my life within the love of God. I might die many more times before my physical existence on this planet comes to an end. But regardless of how many times I die, I know I shall rise again. And the more resurrection becomes a reality in the here and now, the less physical death can at any stage diminish me.

I have ceased trying to work out whether God is interventionist or not. Besides, it makes no sense to say that he intervenes (i.e. comes between). For he is already and constantly 'going between' in the sense that he is intimately and inextricably involved at every level of creative becoming. For the world could not exist at any level without him, being as it is an expression of the outpouring of his life and love.

There are now far more important questions I have to ask, such as 'Why do I find it so difficult to love as Christ calls me to love?' or 'Why do different groups of people find it almost impossible to live peacefully together?'

I suppose I could have gone through life asking all the wrong questions and therefore denied the existence of God. I could have completely ignored his presence in me and everyone else, together with our vocation to labour with him in the garden of his creation. After all, it was much more straightforward to blame God for everything. And it is very much harder to take responsibility for myself. It is quite daunting to think that, in common with my fellow human beings, I am an embodiment of God's energy in the world and in this sense I am living by, with and in the life-giving energies of God.

I used to think I would get to heaven by being kind and considerate to my family and friends. Now I realize that redemption requires, even relies on, how well I know and understand myself. For as my knowledge of myself deepens and develops, the love of God increasingly fills my heart and life.

As my faith continues to fall into place and I look back at my heartfelt protests earlier on, I sometimes find it difficult to recognize myself in that angry and pain-filled person I used to be.

5

Love in person

Different prayers, changed perspective

Moving from protest to a deeper understanding of prayer does not necessarily mean that prayerful protest can never be a legitimate part of the Christian life. But while the impetus of our struggle to make sense of things is often moved by pain and frustration, the context of our praying is faithful rather than fatalistic.

The more I have been able to appreciate and understand how God can be 'all in all', the more I have found my life to be a movement of prayer. As I recall how the Spirit of God is described as wind and breath in the Old and New Testaments, I feel that in every breath I take I cannot help but be involved in the life of God.

Recently, my friend Anne died. Instead of praying that God should let her die or pleading with God that she should live, this time, even though Anne was only in her fifties, I prayed that she might know how to die. And I prayed that I might know how best to support her. I mean, what can you say to someone in such circumstances? I suppose you just hope that rather than any words that might betray you or them, something of the Spirit of Christ seeps out in each encounter.

Anne was a doctor who had spent most of her working life in general practice. She had been forced to take early retirement having been diagnosed with terminal cancer. She was a practising Christian and the need to face her own mortality tested her faith to the limit. As a doctor she had seen death at first hand many times. New questions naturally arose, however, as she experienced the dying process herself. She knew there was to be no remission and I admired her courage as her health deteriorated. She had faith but she wanted to try and understand more.

At her request, I used to take Communion to her house where she, her husband and I would sit in prayer, share bread and wine and sometimes talk about our faith in the face of life and death.

I can remember thinking I had put my foot in it, so to speak, one time soon after I had begun to take them Communion at home. In the form of service I was using, just before the bread and wine are given, everyone is invited to join together and say, 'Lord, I am not worthy to receive you, but only say the word and I shall be healed.' I noticed that my doctor friend who so far had been joining in the service fell silent at this point.

Afterwards she explained to me that she had already prayed for healing and clearly her condition had not improved. She suspected that there was another, greater form of healing that is granted in the next life and it was to this that the words in the service referred. But in case we were being encouraged to focus our attention purely on healing in this life, she thought she would be happier not to join in at this point. So in future services I left the offending sentence out altogether.

The weeks and months passed and the service with its amendment continued, as did our discussions. But it was not long before her body finally succumbed to the disease. Just before she died, her husband asked her if she was afraid of anything. 'No,' she told him, 'What have I to be afraid of? My faith has shown me not only the way to live but also the way to die.'

The darkness that had earlier on threatened to destroy her had gone. She had found an inner healing that was far greater than any pills, potions or earthbound resuscitation could bring about. As her body had become weaker, her spirit had become stronger.

I did not pray that she should know how to die simply because I was at a loss to think of any other way of praying. This prayer was not as a result of some fatalistic acceptance that life and death are unfathomable and that God must know what he is doing even if it makes no sense to me. Instead, the reason that I prayed that she should know how to die was that I could now appreciate how the Spirit of God moves through life and death in a way that I had not understood before.

The point here is that for those who believe in Christ, there is no death that cannot be followed by life. Anne died and rose again some time before her physical demise. And this is true for anyone who becomes thus incorporated into the life of Christ. Alexander Schmemann reminds us:

> For Christianity *help* is not the criterion. The purpose of Christianity is not to help people by reconciling them with death, but to reveal the Truth about life and death in order that people may be saved by this Truth.[1]

In pursuit of this Truth we are called to give ourselves tirelessly to promote justice at the expense of injustice, peace at the expense of war, good at the expense of evil. We work and pray for the healing of creation. Our hope is drawn into a picture of heaven and earth as a garden where once again God and humanity can walk together. In this conflict, it is the amount of creative love we promote, release and en-person that promotes the possibilities of the kingdom more than anything else. What, therefore, brings victory over evil is the degree of love we bring to bear on human and cosmic suffering. In short, the way in which we live and die.

For it is only by love that the world will be redeemed:

> We do not live to ourselves, and we do not die to ourselves. If we live, we live to the Lord, and if we die, we die to the Lord; so then, whether we live or whether we die, we are the Lord's. (Rom. 14.7–8)

So we can no longer speak about death without at the same time speaking about life. Death has indeed lost its sting (1 Cor. 15.55). Here death has been overcome by life, crucifixion by resurrection.

This does not mean that we wish to deny death any of its pain and the brokenness and bewilderment it visits on so many. While I believe strongly in resurrection, I am not one of those people who appear to use their belief in life after death as a cause for celebration and not much else at funerals. Some Christians approach the process of grief with an almost manic religious desire to 'prove' their faith in the face of death. For God's sake, why can we not just be ourselves here, too, and admit openly – even publicly – that death can be extremely traumatic? Our grief for our loved ones can be heart-breaking. Death by itself is dysfunctional. All good people are committed to life, yet death robs the world of life wherever it can. Death deprives the living of life. It crucifies love. Death comes not only to take physical life away in a wooden box but also to do its best to cripple the life that remains.

But the degree to which we are prepared to face the pain probably determines the degree to which we experience the resurrection.

On three occasions in the Gospels Jesus is described as raising people from the dead.[2] In the Fourth Gospel Jesus asks Mary, her brother Lazarus having died, whether or not she believes that her brother will rise again. She says that she knows that he will rise at the resurrection on the last day. This reply does not seem to satisfy Jesus who then says, 'I am the resurrection and the life. Those who believe in me, even though they die, will live, and everyone who lives and believes in me will never die' (John 11.25). The resurrection that follows death takes place in the context of the resurrection of life in the here and now.

Jesus is not pictured as raising Lazarus from the dead simply to prove that God has the power to do so, nor simply to prefigure his own eventual resurrection. If this were the case, his action would have been the equivalent of a supernatural stunt. This was not an option for Christ as we see in his refusal to be tempted to throw himself off the highest point of the Temple and be saved from death by his angels (Matt. 4.5–6). The point here is that, quite simply, for those who believe in Christ there is no death that cannot be followed by life.

Jesus Christ brings the power of resurrection into the present. He speaks not only in terms of the future but also of the continuous present, as if the one is to be found in the other. While creation heads to a point of spiritual union with the Creator, in the meantime the consummation of everything is made available at least to some degree in the present. The early Church thought for a while that the end of the world was imminent until they discovered that the end had already taken place and the new age had begun. This way of seeing things, of course, is the only way to relate to God, who while being intimately involved in creation is in essence timeless.

So while we face up to the pain of death and the suffering it causes, we can also experience – maybe at the same time – a peace and a sense of eternity in the face of it.

Therefore, wherever physical, emotional or spiritual death takes place, there is the possibility for new life now. There is no need to run from these matters any more; no requirement to speak in hushed tones about something we try to avoid at all costs. Instead, contrary to our natural inclinations, we can discover that by embracing death in all its many forms – rather than being dominated by it – we can find new life.

Amid suffering and pain we know that love overcomes hatred, and life is stronger than death. In the cold and merciless setting of the survival of the fittest, we can work with the Spirit of Christ in a counter-cultural way to bring good news to the poor, to proclaim release to the captives, recovery of sight to the blind and to set free the oppressed (Luke 4.18).

We cannot fulfil God's purpose for our lives if we see fulfilment as something that only comes after the end of our physical existence. This seems to be one of those laws of evolution that applies also to our spiritual lives. For if we are not prepared to grow, adapt and develop in the here and now we will die . . . along with our religion, because a life-less faith makes little contact with reality.

Growing up, though, can be painful, because in growing up we have to take increasing responsibility for ourselves.

Growing up

Some people have to grow up more quickly than others. Young children who are orphaned in war, for example, find themselves with adult responsibilities from an early age. Others grow up too slowly. Too much security and the wrong kind of love in the developing years can lead to a dependence upon the dynamics of family life to the extent that they find it difficult to be at home in adult relationships.

Then there are those who do not appear to grow up at all. They remain locked in child-like behaviour as a result perhaps of some kind of abuse earlier on or an overriding need for personal security. These good people are never able to take full responsibility for who they are.

There is, of course, no single proven or guaranteed way of growing up. Most of us do it in fits and starts. How we react to our various experiences of life determines to what degree we develop. So rather than taking full responsibility for our lives at one particular time, we tend to achieve our aim by stages and according to the degree we are prepared to grow in understanding ourselves.

Baptism is not a guarantee that we will remain unbuffeted by the world all our lives. As infants, usually, we are baptized into the death and resurrection of Jesus Christ (Rom. 6.4a). Here we are moved by his Spirit to become engaged with the growth and development of love against the friction of the world's godlessness.

This friction can simultaneously make us more rounded as individuals and knock chunks off us. And it is at times difficult to work out which aspects of our inherited patterns of belief and ecclesiastical structures we need to leave behind. As soon as we question the teaching we have received, we can put ourselves at odds with some of the teaching of the Church.

In my own case, I have come to the conclusion that my understanding of the meaning of Christ and the Christian faith – which is at odds with the institutional and fairly rigid model we work with most of the time – is much closer to the faith of the early Church of the East than I had previously thought.

It is time to admit that we need to lose the version of Christianity that Western consumerism has produced. If we fail do so there are those who are sure that, sooner or later, the Church will die.

This process of growing up is helped greatly by the fact that we are more prepared to express our feelings today than certainly was the case when I was a child in the 1950s. And because we are more self-aware, a Church that treats its members as children – with its emphasis on obedience, prohibitions and discipline – will be regarded by society as an inhibitor rather than a facilitator of self-awareness and the processes that lead to personal maturity.

One of the positive and healthy consequences of moving from a hierarchical, paternalistic model to one that is centred more on the 'individual in community with others' is that – as we have seen – we are far less likely to have a theology of prayer that consists of asking God to mend the ills of the world. Instead, we understand more fully the importance of learning how we can mend ourselves and take more responsibility for change and the incarnation of Christ in ourselves and our communities.

When Jesus was preparing his disciples for his absence, he told them that they would grow to know that 'I am in my Father, and you in me, and I in you' (John 14.20). So by taking responsibility for ourselves we are taking responsibility for

Christ. And when we take responsibility for Christ we are able to reveal his love to the world.

We cannot underestimate the importance of each individual's calling to fulfil his or her potential. The word 'potential' comes from a Latin word meaning 'power', and discovering 'Christ in me and myself in Christ' is immensely empowering.

As the Spirit leads us further into the Truth, we receive power to believe in ourselves and move on. With this power comes the freedom to love in new and better ways or maybe even to discover authentic love for the first time. The guilt that prevents the healing and balanced development of our love need not shackle us to the sins of the past. Didn't Jesus tell his disciples that the truth he would reveal would set them free (John 8.31)?

The consequence of this for the Church is that when individual Christians are set free in this way, they become far less interested in the failure of others and more committed to their healing.

The Church of England has only recently decided to accept the remarriage of divorcees.[3] Even now that clergy can go ahead with such services, there are some clergy and laity who are unable to accept that this ministry is valid. And even some of those who do take such services can be quite judgemental in their approach and attitude because of precise points of theology and biblical interpretation. Add to this current debates concerning gay rights and the equality of men and women within the Church and you can see the sort of mess you are bound to end up with when you allow the Christian faith to become more of a religion than a Way of life and when you permit the Church to become an end in itself, where holding on to structures becomes more important than letting go in love. The parable of the Pharisee and the Tax-collector springs to mind (Luke 18.10–14).

However, the fact that the Church has now decided to permit the remarriage of divorcees is for me an indication that the spiritual torpor and general decline from which the Church has been suffering for many years is coming to an end. It is a signal of the rebirth of the faith. It means that we have begun to rediscover our ability to recognize Christ in others and in particular among those where love has not turned out as expected. It signifies that we have begun to exchange the rules of ecclesiastical law for the kingdom of love. In short, we are growing up again. I am hopeful, therefore, that the community of faith will not die, as some fear, but live.

Such a challenge to the institution can be frightening and forbidding. It is easier to play by the rules. Not just in the matter of the remarriage of those who have been divorced but in our discussions concerning gay rights and the place of women in the Church. In many ways we would prefer that others made the decisions for us. Love can be indefinable and intangible. It often asks questions we would rather not have to answer. It demands that we grow with every decision we make, every additional piece of information we acquire. Love admits us to uncharted waters. Most of all, love requires that we get to know ourselves more and more, again and again.

A faith that provides us with clear, rigid unchangeable definitions concerning what is right and wrong, a purpose and direction for our lives and an assurance that in the end 'all will be well' has a high survival attraction. However, as I read the Gospels, it was not the intention of Jesus Christ that the Christian faith should offer this kind of suffocating certainty. And this is surely one of its strengths. It speaks more in terms of exploration, with an emphasis on the need for self-understanding. It does not at first appear to be efficient or even relevant for the binding together of a group, or nation. But when it is hijacked by politicians, both inside the Church and outside, it becomes a grotesque caricature of what it is supposed to be. So it is unsurprising, then, that the freedom to love can quickly be suffocated by the need to survive.

We can see now why Christianity and other religions have had such a heavy-handed approach to human sexuality and why the sexual revolution of the 1960s has had such an undermining effect on the life of the Church. For 'religions are the earliest cultural systems, of which we have evidence, for the protection of gene replication and the nurture of children'.[4] And we no longer need religion to tell us what we can and cannot do in terms of gene replication, food distribution and child-rearing.

Religions in general and Christianity in particular have in the past played a vital role in species preservation and development, not least in areas of group identity, resources acquisition, mate selection and retention, health promotion and the structured organization of society based on well-defined roles for men and women. Here again is evidence of how in a fallen world of competing lures, the Spirit of love emerges slowly and often painfully. We observe how the Christian faith has often been absorbed into religious systems that have been largely determined by the laws of evolutionary survival. This is why some more fundamentalist versions of the faith are so attractive to those for whom survival is the dominant driving force in their lives. This is as true for some church growth in the poorer parts of Africa[5] – where scant resources and violence threaten life daily – as it is in those places where rich young people have sold out to Western materialism. The materialists – whose aim is also to survive at all costs in a different but nonetheless highly competitive world – miss the point that the Christian faith is not primarily about evolutionary survival but about promoting 'life in all its fullness' (John 10.10). For when the human spirit is energized by the Holy Spirit it is no longer orientated around the selfish acquisition of resources – material and spiritual – but, instead, addresses the needs of the hungry, naked, homeless and marginalized.

The nature of the Holy Spirit – as we have seen – is not to confirm our natural instincts but to confront them with unconditional and sacrificial love. And it is precisely because the Church has become so preoccupied – some might say obsessed – with organized religion that it cannot relate easily or readily to what the Spirit is up to in the world. Hence the dreadfully demeaning attitude the Church has towards the gay community, while people outside the Church generally are much more spiritually aware in these issues, having as they do a far more enlightened understanding and approach to gay issues.

There are, of course, those within the Church for whom faith is more important than religion, but unfortunately this still small voice of the Divine presence within the Christian community is not always heard, and listened to even less. For some reason we are reluctant to learn profound lessons about our relationship with society from the religion-less communities of Christian faith, such as Taizé and the community of Aidan and Hilda on Holy Island, which actually achieve the right balance between faithful prayer and the freedom of the Spirit. Instead we tend to use them for occasional recreation instead, reducing their contribution to the status of coffee-table Christianity.

So even now as the Church is setting up mission-shaped communities in clubs and pubs, in some cases it does not recognize the false dualism it perpetuates between what it understands as its ownership of Jesus Christ and the Christ who belongs to creation. Sometimes you will find the Church trying to build bridges between itself and society without realizing that what it is offering is fundamentally the same religion of evolutionary survival that exists in society. It would do better to concentrate on helping people to have faith in themselves and to fulfil the purposes of God in their lives for the good of creation.

I dare say that there will be those who will say that a life of faith such as I have suggested is impractical and idealistic to the point of bordering on sheer fantasy. For by and large we need our evolutionary reference points as individuals and also in the Church and society. We need the rule of law to protect the innocent.

I would agree with them to the extent that in a fallen world it would be incredibly naive, irresponsible, if not plain stupid, to think that everyone could suddenly be able to live as Christ lived. But surely it is not impossible for the Christian disciple to live by this kind of unconditional love as the leaven in a society governed by law (Matt. 13.33).

Meeting Christ

John Main reminds us that in nature, growth is from the centre outwards.[6] While we may lose sight of this from time to time, it has always been true since the earliest days of Christian discipleship that we become Christ-like not by being externally religious but by making an interior journey.

As the sacraments of self-denial that lead to self-annihilation are replaced by the self-offering that leads to a Spirit-filled life, I am drawn to the Christ who promotes my self-awareness so that I can understand increasingly who I am.

As I contemplate the meaning of 'God with us' as proclaimed by the Church especially at Christmas, it occurs to me that the nearest I have ever been to meeting Christ has been through the love of others. It is the effect of their love on me that makes the difference. It is not just that we are meant to fulfil our human potential but that, as we do this, we reveal more of the God who is within us all.

I discover him, for example, in the patient, listening and affirming presence of someone who provides me with an environment secure enough for me to confront and overcome my own 'demons'. These 'demons' are known by their fake spirituality that disrupts the image of Christ within me. And as they depart I begin to recognize Christ as the one who is at the centre of who I am.

I see him also in the miracle of a newborn child, an unmistakable yet inexpressible consciousness of eternity that makes you look into the eyes of a baby and say, 'You were the last to see him. What did God say to you before he sent you here from that place where one day I, too, will watch you?'

It is crazy to think that we lose sight of God simply by being weak and fallible. Otherwise the penitent thief would not have recognized Christ on the cross next to him. God made us with the potential both to promote love and to cause suffering. So he accepts – though does not condone – that we are very likely to promote both love and pain in a world that has fallen away from its original orbit around the heart of authentic love.

We do lose sight of God, however, when we actively engage against the emergence of the Spirit of creative love in us and in the world. Despite his encounter with Christ on the cross next to him, the impenitent thief chose death rather than life. This is something we are happy to do more than we would care to admit. We suffocate the Spirit in creation by our irresponsible custodianship of its resources. We suppress the presence of Christ in human nature by our inability to escape sufficiently our biologically driven nature.

This is why the sin against the Holy Spirit is the one and only unforgivable sin (Mark 3.29). For to live disengaged from the creative source of life in the universe is to live apart from God. Such an existence of self-interest can only be lived at the expense of others' freedom and well-being and at the expense of God. For a while it may be attractive – even fun – to decide to distance oneself from God. But there is no hope of eternity here, only degrees of self-destruction.

We tend to interpret sin against God predominantly in terms of immoral behaviour. But sin – literally 'missing the target' or a failure to fulfil our divine potential – means much more than this.

Sin is not only a refusal to grow (into the likeness of God) but is also the idea that we can either 'use' God for our evolutionary survival or do without him at all. This has been Adam's (humanity's) mistake. Refusing to enhance the progress of the Spirit of life, we separate ourselves from the source of all life and love.

To enter into the Spirit-filled life requires energy and persistence, together with the willingness to put up with some pain. But if we can find the way through we will find an ecstasy, a beauty, a peace beyond understanding where earth and heaven meet. For when we discover the still small voice of self-acceptance and understanding – purified of the driven will of selfish motives – we find ourselves in the eternal present. With hearts reclaimed from survival and defence imperatives, we are able to see God both within and beyond.

Nothing can take away this ecstasy or the experience of loving and being loved that it bestows. Even when love grows cold, the memory of the intimacy of the naked embrace between Divine and human spirit keeps alive the fire of life that burns both in stars and hearts.

While I discover truth in the necessary friction between myself and the fissures and fractures of the world and human relationships, the end of this endeavour is not burn-out or black hole. It is, instead, a way of loving so beautiful that it becomes the pearl of great price (Matt. 13.45–46) for which I would give everything.

So it is love – rather than guilt – that develops our self-image. It enables us to connect, to harmonize, to stay in touch, to find eternity in ordinary things.

Our experience of the garden is not one of unbroken harmony with the source and principles of life that produce only beauty. Instead, we labour under the heat of the summer sun and the cold of the winter to encourage life to break through among the thistles and weeds of worldly existence.

A leading figure in the early Church once said that the 'glory of God is a human being fully alive'.[7] I understand this to mean 'fully alive to the possibilities and potential of creative love in all things'. For this glory cannot be privatized for the benefit of an individual. Instead, the presence of God can only be fully appreciated in a person's life as he or she relates to their environment, to creation as well as to others.

Some people behave as if church buildings and the religious objects within them are the only places that are sacred. But the presence of the Spirit within all created reality renders the world itself sacred. The way we react to – the way we treat and live within – this environment where creative love emerges, therefore, is either sacrilegious or the way of sanctification.

This depends upon whether our actions enhance or deny the life of the Spirit. But even when we have opted for life over death, we have to continue to be faithful if things are to turn out right in the end. Like the intimacy of the lover's kiss, the experience of eternity runs alongside the risk of that betrayal that will attempt to deny us our very selves.

Christ came that we might have life 'abundantly' and enjoy it free from prejudice. But the Church can induce spiritual depression by refusing to allow the Spirit to overcome our natural tendencies to want power, position and physical security.

I visited a church recently and remarked to one of the congregation how beautiful it was inside. She replied that it had been better before 'they took the pews out'. She made me think that in her mind at least the kingdom had extended only as far as church furniture. She reminded me of a church meeting where the people began every sentence with the word 'I', not as an expression of Godly identity but to assert themselves and make their bid for power.

God forgive those Christians who in countless ways impose their own agendas upon the gospel of Jesus Christ without even a nod in his direction or an ear even half open to his word. It wouldn't be so bad if it stopped here, for we would be condemning only ourselves. Tragically, as we prevent the Divine incarnation in ourselves, we deny the opportunities for his 'fullness of life' to others.

When we privatize the Holy Spirit we condemn both the Church and the world to the politics of survival.

It is one and the same Spirit who beckons all things at every level of created existence – once shattered but now moving towards greater levels of fulfilment – to find their identity and purpose within God. It is also the Spirit of life moving through the mission of Christ who brings new life and meaning to a world of broken relationships. It was the continuous and total possession of Jesus by the Spirit that convinced his followers that he was not only the Messiah but also the Son of God.

In English, Greek and Hebrew the same word can be used to describe human spirit and the life-giving and renewing power of the Spirit of God. In both Old and New Testaments there are occasions when it is difficult to decipher whether what is being referred to is the Spirit of God or the spirit of human beings. What we are seeing here are various authors struggling to find a way of describing how God transcends the human self while also being within it.

It is here that I find the uniqueness of Christ. Not so much in what he said and did, for there are strong parallel sayings and miracles performed in other religious traditions. Not so much in the fact that he is referred to as the Son of God, conceived outside the normal means of childbirth. In themselves these are faithful ways of saying that Jesus was the promised One given to the world by God. To this extent their historical validity is second to the profundity of spiritual statement found within these terms, sayings and activity.

Whichever myth we may opt for, the Truth is that his life was lived in such a way that it became uncontaminated by spiritual fallout. His uniqueness is that 'at the right time' Christ became what has been described in theological/scientific terms as 'the mutation of love to reveal the goal of evolution'.[8] In the words of the myth, Paul expresses it like this:

> So with us; while we were minors, we were enslaved to the elemental spirits of the world. But when the fullness of time had come, God sent his Son, born of a woman, born under the law . . . so that we might receive adoption as children.

> And because you are children, God has sent the Spirit of his Son into our hearts, crying, 'Abba! Father!' (Gal. 4.3–6)

Against the background of the mission of creative love following the pre-universal Fall, the Spirit in the life of Jesus reaches a fullness of expression unknown either before or since.

The uniqueness of Christ is first and foremost in his spiritual identity, that is, an unrestricted fusion of Spirit and matter. Here heaven and earth, fullness of God and fullness of humanity, are held together at the centre by the heart of Creative Love itself.

The life of Jesus is 'the life of heaven on earth'. In this incarnation of the unconditional love of God, humanity is offered the possibility of its own unequivocal 'yes' to the lure of love. Our salvation, therefore, consists of being caught up in this love – letting it loose in ourselves – as we seek to 'imitate' the example of the second Adam, the archetype of the new human being. He is the person in whose likeness we are meant to grow and develop. We are called to become Christ ourselves.

When St Paul describes the development of the Christian in terms of being transformed from one degree of glory to another (2 Cor. 3.18), we can understand that this refers to the Spirit of love filling a person's life to an ever-increasing degree.

While Paul can describe the natural human condition in terms of everyone having 'fallen short' (Rom. 3.23) of this glory, the word 'glory' here refers to the visible expression of the fullness of the love of God. The glory of God becomes real in the world as death is overcome by life, hell is overcome by heaven. This is why, just before raising Lazarus, Jesus twice tells his followers that his friend has died in order that the glory of God might be made known to this world (John 11.4, 40).

St Paul summarizes what this means for the individual Christian as follows: 'If the Spirit of him who raised Jesus from the dead dwells in you, he who raised Christ from the dead will give life to your mortal bodies also through his Spirit that dwells in you' (Rom. 8.11).

At the beginning of John's Gospel, Jesus is described as the Word of God, the utterance of the mind of God in human form, the incarnation of his creative love. This we have come to know is a creative Word of understanding, encouragement and hope, which banishes the darkness of confusion and self-doubt. It is also the Word that transforms our selfish preoccupation with survival at all costs into a self-sufficiency in the Spirit.

The Church renders Jesus remote from the human experience of the rest of us when it interprets the sinlessness of Christ in terms of a faultlessness from the beginning. Here Christ deals with the wounds of the world on the cross as unblemished sacrifice. But surely this kind of delivered perfection leaves him (w)holy removed from the lives of ordinary people.

If he truly was a human being as the fulfilment of the process of becoming divine, this means that he, like us, was wounded in the sense that he had to deal with all the normal baggage we acquire through our upbringing as we grow by degrees into becoming the offspring of God. While the Church came to know him as the Son of God, he called himself Son of Man.[9]

We have come to realize that the words 'by his wounds we are healed' refer not only to those wounds inflicted upon Jesus on the cross but also to those he suffered before the final act of his Passion. The blood that falls from his broken body on Skull Hill outside Jerusalem is the climax of all the suffering and godforsakenness that has gone before.

His sacrifice is therefore unblemished not because of some vertical descent from heavenly places but by the purity of the unconditional love by which it was surrendered in the service of humanity. The source of his life was found in the heart of the creative love of God. This is why he could also be described as the 'lamb who was slain from the foundation of the world' (Rev. 13.8). In him we see the fulfilment of the love of God that was present before the pre-universal Fall. He offers a model of pre-fallen relationships both human, Divine and in creation. And, as we have seen, our life comes from the same source, so we may assert that God 'chose us in Christ before the foundation of the world to be holy and blameless before him in love' (Eph. 1.4).

'Sinless' here does not mean that Jesus was unaffected by the world to the point of surgical sterility but that he consistently met evil with the love of his Spirit.

Jesus knew this evil through the frustration that comes from being misunderstood by many and even by those closest to him, his family and his disciples. He was greatly disturbed and wept when he came to the tomb of Lazarus. He wept over Jerusalem's failure to pursue love rather than power. He felt the rejection of the religious people who – above all others – should have accepted him. He knew the struggle that we go through when we have to oppose evil. And he experienced those feelings of abandonment and estrangement from God which come at times of extreme pain and suffering.

The power of creative love in him, therefore, is unique in that its fullness was and is present wherever we are now and one day seek to be. Creative love cannot operate through those who become self-righteous in their religion. It works most powerfully in those who know they have been crippled by good processes that have turned out wrong. As we come to realize that we are wounded, we can be healed by the Spirit of Christ.

Here the rules of evolutionary survival are reversed. The dinner gong goes and the weak shuffle, stagger and struggle their way into the room – the poor, the crippled, the blind and the lame – to sit at the messianic Banquet.[10] Those who had invitations – the self-righteous religious people who think they are healthy – have made their excuses. They are elsewhere. Absent. In their place there is an unlikely band of battered people now being made whole, brought together from the highways and byways of life. They are not there because they feel they have earned the right to sit at the table by using the sacraments of the Church to amass a sufficient score of good deeds. They know themselves too well for that. Instead, they know they are there by grace alone. Around this table there is no self-righteous rejoicing that they have made it 'in', that ignores the plight of those who are 'out'. Just a simple and quiet acceptance of where they are, coupled with a deep sense of gratitude for the love that has got them there.[11]

God will complete his plan when the time is right. This has been described as a time when he will 'gather up all things in [Christ], things in heaven and things on earth' (Eph. 1.9–10). This will be accomplished through an undistinguished and unlikely band of people, the Church, whose members make up the mystical Body of Christ, 'the fullness of him who fills all in all' (Eph. 1.23). So the Church, in the words of Alexander Schmemann, is the sacrament of the kingdom not because she possesses divinely instituted acts such as baptism and the Eucharist but because 'first of all she is the possibility given to man to see in and through this world the "world to come," to see it and to "live" it in Christ'.[12]

God in Christ calls us, therefore, to take responsibility for our spiritual journey as we are called to replace the instincts of survival with the embodiment of love.

Becoming Christ

Finding out who you are inevitably entails working on who you are meant to become. The meaning of the passage from Paul's letter to the Galatians (Gal. 4.1–7), to which I referred in the last chapter (pp. 141–2) in the light of the pre-fallen universe myth, could be interpreted to read as follows:

> At the right time in the process of the emergence of love in creation, God sent the Spirit of his Son into our hearts so that we might no longer be slaves to evolutionary

necessity. Instead, as our wills become free from our earthly passions, the Spirit of Christ increasingly fills our lives. As a result we are adopted into the Godhead where our inheritance of unrestricted access to the Father of us all is regained. By such grace we begin to learn how to love again in this world. But this time without conditions.

If I am called to be free rather than a slave, I need first to think about what it is that will make me free. If it is not primarily to do with an austerity of lifestyle then what does it consist of? I now realize that freedom does not come simply from what you give up but from who you are. While Francis of Assisi, to whom I referred earlier, is renowned for the way in which he forsook the comforts of this world, he was renewed most of all by his desire to reinvent himself in Christ.[13]

Francis took Jesus as his model of the one who was completely at peace with himself. There could have been no room for dishonesty in Jesus' personal feelings and inclinations. Nor would there have been any room for false dualisms either between himself and other people or himself and the world. His spirit and the emotional and mental sides of his character were integrated into a wholeness of being.

If Jesus was completely at one with himself, it follows that he must have been completely at one with the God who is the ground of human being and becoming. As a result of this integration Jesus was able to speak of God as his Father.

But if I wish to pursue this way of freedom, I need to know whether it is possible for me, too, to become a new person in Christ? And if so, how would I describe the process by which I achieve this?

When Jesus is praying for his disciples before he is arrested and taken away from them he says, 'As you, Father, are in me and I am in you, may they also be in us' (John 17.21). These words remind us of the contrast between the words of the misguided people in my church meeting who began every sentence with the word 'I' and the way in which, particularly in the Fourth Gospel, Jesus prefaces the descriptions of his spiritual life with the words 'I am'. For example, 'I am the resurrection and the life' (John 11.25), or 'I am the way, and the truth, and the life' (John 14.6) and so on.

The focus of the word of the people is 'I', while the context of the word of Jesus is 'I am'. We might be forgiven for thinking this is only a small and insignificant point. But nothing could be further from the Truth. For here is nothing less than the difference between evolutionary self-interest and revolutionary love in human being and becoming.

The Hebrew name by which God famously reveals himself to Moses – YHWEH – means 'I AM WHO I AM' (Exod. 3.14). Given what we have noted about the 'I am' of Jesus Christ, we can see that in both Jewish and Christian faith, God is to be found as the basis of all identity and being. He who is himself continuous being is also the 'I am' in the essence of all existence. Of all creation, though, only humanity can consciously recognize and fully respond to this 'I am' because of our 'higher' powers of reasoning and reflective thought.

To become increasingly aware of who I am, therefore, is to become more aware of – and therefore closer to – my Creator. To know Christ as the Divine 'I am' in me is to know the God who lives in me.

The sacramental principle that the incarnation reveals is not that certain special sacraments suspend the natural laws of life to reveal the power and presence of God in supernatural ways. Instead, the principle behind the incarnation is that all life is sacramental. Jesus, therefore, shows us how to embrace our divinity. And, indeed, the divinity of the world.

Jesus frequently uses the words 'I am' to denote this Divine potential. Written in Greek, the language of the New Testament, the words used for 'I am' are *ego eimi*. Different psychologists, of course, describe the role of the ego in human behaviour in different ways. For me, my ego is the place where my will is situated and where my passion for life becomes conscious. My ego is my natural self. It is the 'I' in me. It is driven largely by biologically determined and culturally conditioned impulses which are concerned with self-interest and survival.

My ego is my unredeemed self. Me without my divinity recognized. My ego can produce great kindness within groups that do not threaten me. It can even produce a kind of loving as a result of reason and rationality, but not by divinity. My ego can also be base and rude. For here is where my drive to survive gives expression in my daily conduct. It is the place where I get on at the expense of others. This is where 'I' display my natural self-centredness. Here I sometimes mutate my views and feelings – even if it means denying my integrity – in order to get the most out of my surroundings and others.

However, while my ego behaves according to my human nature within its evolutionary environment, it is also the place where truth and authentic love emerge. In the evolution of my fallen self, love surfaces usually as a result of the Spirit's emergence through my subconscious self. Thrusting its way to the surface in a similar manner to the way in which I earlier described the Spirit surfacing through creation, it is helped or hindered, celebrated or crucified, by my own willingness or recalcitrance to grow towards spiritual maturity.

Most of us most of the time operate only at the level of the ego. 'I' tend to do what 'I' want to do. 'I' relate to others according to how 'I' understand them. We can fool ourselves that the ego is our authentic self. When we do this, we produce a fake divinity. We become comfortable with our instinctual behaviour, which we frequently confirm by using the institution of the Church to make our godlessness respectable.

This should not surprise us. For it is much more straightforward to live with the ego preserved. To do so, however, is to deny Divinity its place in evolution. But wherever human beings begin to put their conditioned patterns of behaviour into the context of creative love, we see the Spirit of Christ emerging.

As a Christian I would describe the process by which I come to be 'in Christ' as being about how the ego – the 'I' of fallen human identity – becomes the *ego eimi*, the 'I am' of the Spirit-filled Christ.

As I become attuned to and actively promote the life of the Spirit of Christ within me, my ego becomes by stages the *ego eimi* of God. No longer 'I' but 'I am', where 'I' represents a refusal to change and grow and 'I am' represents a commitment to become the person God has called me to be in the fulfilment of my divine potential. Paul expressed this more fully by saying, 'I have been crucified with Christ; and it is no longer I who live, but it is Christ who lives in me' (Gal. 2.20).

For those who seek this kind of growth into God, life is likely to become more complicated. My Christian faith exposes me to the restlessness of eternity. I find myself constantly questioning my behaviour and wrestling with the inequalities of life. Resurrection is a counter-culture in a world that has yet to be redeemed. While my new-found knowledge of God grants a spiritual peace beyond all understanding (Phil. 4.7), the practice of my life of prayer can be full of pain.

For the Spirit of creative love confronts anything that inhibits the Spirit's growth in myself, others and in creation. It reveals the prejudices of my conditioned behaviour for what they are. It moves restlessly over the waters of my soul demanding that I change. Its hope is that I am driven by my divinity and desire to be united with God rather than the demons of my earthly survival won at the expense of others. It longs for my life to turn out right in the end.

To understand fully the implications of the life and teaching of Christ is to appreciate their significance in the revelation of God in the history of the emergence of creative love and the evolution of the planet.

The ministry of Jesus can be divided broadly into two sections. First, his work in the Galilean countryside and, second, his ministry in Jerusalem. There are considerable differences between the two and by looking at these we can further contextualize his ministry and its implications for the beckoning 'I am' in humanity.

In Galilee, Jesus is free of the constraints of the institution. He calls for the religious establishment to be changed as the new wine of his kingdom cannot fit into the old wineskins (Mark 2.22). He preaches a new way of life based on who he is and who you and I can become. Here we can see how the Spirit of Christ confronts the survival imperatives of fallen human nature. Standing in the synagogue in Capernaum not far from the shore of Lake Galilee, he describes the source of nourishment for this way of living by saying, 'I am the living bread that came down from heaven. Whoever eats of this bread will live for ever' (John 6.51a).

Jesus teaches not only in synagogues but also on hillsides and by the seashore. Here in Galilee, the temple that is the centre of his faith is not the magnificent religious building in Jerusalem. Instead, it is the human being who is the temple of the Holy Spirit. The more this temple is filled with the Spirit of Christ, the more the renewed human being enjoys life in Christ in all its fullness (John 10.10). This is a theme that St Paul picks up later and advocates to all Christians.[14]

The people come out from the countryside and villages to be with him. They bring their sick with them and lay them at his feet. Or they bring them to the door of the house where he is staying that he might heal them. They long for spiritual nourishment. They want to hear the words that give life. The poor have few vested interests. Consequently, they are less likely to be made to feel insecure by the demands of love. They have little to lose. They want to reach out and touch him so that their lives might become whole, too.

It is not long, however, before we see that Jesus' understanding of the gospel stands in stark contrast to those who have vested interests in the survival of the religious establishment. These people are concentrated in Jerusalem. When they first hear of Jesus they send some of their number to check him out, to see if he poses a threat to their institutionalized security. They find that he does. So the stage is set, early on, for that final phase of his ministry when Jesus enters Jerusalem for the last time.

Clearly, those who have allowed their faith to become enslaved to the politics of survival are threatened by the freedom of the Spirit exhibited in the life of Jesus of Nazareth. Those whose fulfilment is found in the unredeemed needs of the ego will only surrender their security with the greatest reluctance. They have no wish to acknowledge a way of life that is not central to – let alone denies – the ambitions of the ego.

We have noted that religions can perform a species-preserving function in the way that they codify and pass on vital information from one generation to another.[15] Religious leaders and their political counterparts know both the positive and negative aspects of how this species-preserving aspect can be used. On the one hand, it can act as a cohesive force for national identity. On the other hand, it can perpetuate endless inter-tribal or inter-national hostility.

Jesus spoke, therefore, not in the hushed tones of compromise but as a revolutionary. He was a Galilean whose purity of spirit stood in direct contradiction to those whose God was defined by human nature; God made in the image of humanity. This is why Jesus was executed. But here is also the reason why his story did not end on the cross. For his was the revolution of emerging love. His resurrection was guaranteed and universal, for it is none other than the sum of the life of God in human nature.

The religious leaders' response in Galilee is fascinating. They set out to demolish who Jesus is. They try their best to regulate him into non-existence. They reply to his 'I am' with 'No, you are not'. They accuse Jesus of being unlearned, immoral, violent and blasphemous. He is seen as having put himself outside the realm of organized, inherited religion. He eats with sinners, does not observe the religious law and refers to God as being within himself rather than in the incense-filled Holy of Holies in the Jerusalem Temple.

This rejection of Jesus in Galilee reveals the first of two evolutionary survival imperatives at work in human behaviour, both of which promote the selfish needs of the ego against the spiritual demands of the *ego eimi*. The opponents of Jesus have inherited from their ancestors an impulse that stems from our need to maintain our security by denigrating others who threaten us.

My primitive nature encourages me to regard those who compete with me for the same resources as being less good than myself. In extreme circumstances, if it helps me achieve my aims, I might even regard them as demonic or as being less human than I am. Once I have been able to convince myself that such people are in fact my enemies and evil as well, I can justify treating them however I like. At this point love and reconciliation go out of the window as I declare war on my aggressors.

To illustrate what I mean, let me rehearse another well-known story from the gospel.

In Jesus' day, the Samaritans were hated by the orthodox religious Jews. The reason was that these Jews who lived in Samaria were thought to have diluted the pure blood of the chosen race by intermarrying with foreigners, Assyrians, who came to occupy the land. They had betrayed God. But, in fact, all the Samaritans had done was to adapt so that their enemies could become their friends. As a consequence they had ensured their peaceful survival by intermarriage and the mixing of genes.

In the process, of course, they had weakened the genetic base of those members of the nation who had stayed together in exile in a foreign country. Now that the Jews had returned, they were living alongside the Samaritans and competed for the same resources. The Samaritans were therefore a threat to the stability and survival of the Jewish nation. So it is unsurprising to find that the Jews hated them. However, this hatred became more justified and even respectable when overlaid – consciously or subconsciously – by religious justification. As I say, if you think you have God on your side, you can justify even genocide.

Probably the best-known story involving a Samaritan is the parable about a good man from Samaria. People tend to interpret its message in terms of neighbourliness. The 'godless foreigner' (rather than the two Jewish priests who ignored him) acted as a neighbour to the man who lay unconscious by the side of the road, having been robbed.

There is another meaning to this story, however. Dare I say it is the 'real' one? We tend to ignore it because the questions it raises make for uncomfortable thinking! The point here is not primarily about being a good neighbour to everyone, a rather safe and anodyne concept in this instance. Instead, the story points out how religions become meaningless when they put self-preservation above salvation, politics above redemption.

The priest and Levite ignored the dying man for religious reasons. They were both on their way to serve in the Temple. He looked as if he were dead. If they touched him, they would be banned from serving in the Temple because they would have become ritually unclean. Or, if they stopped to help him, they might have been delayed or even beaten up themselves, thereby losing their turn to serve in the Temple.

The Good Samaritan stopped because he was able to put his own religious and national interests second to the need to offer help and support to someone in need. His life was not tied in to a temple cult but he still had a lot to lose. There was nothing for him to gain other than the knowledge that the man he was helping would be looked after and would in all probability recover from his wounds. But deciding to stop would have been contrary to all his survival instincts. It wouldn't have been in his nature. For by stopping, he made himself vulnerable to ambush and attack.

In the Gospels, wherever the Samaritans are mentioned by Christ, their spirituality is held up as an example for others to emulate (Luke 10.29–37; 17.16; John 8.48). This is because the particular Samaritans chosen provide good examples of the positive things that happen when we allow creative love to confront evolutionary drives. Among the Samaritans as a whole Jesus finds people who are not evil but deeply spiritual. They worship God on a different hill to the one on which the Temple is built in Jerusalem but they are nevertheless created by the same loving God as everybody else.

There can be no room for the mindless denigration of others in the kingdom of God so that we can achieve our own ends. As soon as we realize that the basis of our being is not ego but *ego eimi*, we recognize the Divine spiritual ground of all being and becoming in human existence that cuts right across religions and national boundaries. St Paul describes this in his day by saying that here in the Divine economy of relationships, 'there is no longer Greek and Jew, circumcised and uncircumcised, barbarian, Scythian, slave and free; but Christ is all and in all!' (Col. 3.11).

We cannot escape the conclusion that in everyone we encounter we meet with Jesus Christ, and how we react to others has an effect on him. As he says, 'Just as you did [did not do] it to one of . . . these, you did [did not do] it to me' (Matt. 25.40 [45]). This means that having taken responsibility for who we are, we should do everything in our power to help others take responsibility for who they are, too. To promote this process is to promote eternal life (literally life lived in the presence of God, both in this world and the next). By frustrating this process, we bring dislocation from the Divine on ourselves. This is life lived outside the presence of God in this world and the next (Matt. 25.46).

I can now understand more fully why Jesus tells us to love our enemies and pray for those who persecute us (Matt. 5.44). He is not simply asking us to be nice to one another. He is asking so much more. He is beckoning us to release the creative power that can transcend narrow religious boundaries and bring about the completion of creation.

To set the Spirit of creative love free in this way is to recognize the world as the Church and to see Christ in everyone. Olivier Clément writes: 'Wherever the Spirit is at work in history and in the universe, the Church is secretly present.'[16]

Moving on, Jesus confronted the second survival imperative, namely territoriality, in the second part of his ministry as he travelled from Galilee to Jerusalem.

We all know that humans and animals are territorial by nature. Here my ego frequently exerts the strongest pressure. But sometimes I overlook – or even forget altogether – how important a part this plays in my life. Sometimes, unwittingly, we are caught up in such inner drives with the best of intentions, while on other occasions we cynically exploit them for our own ends.

Territoriality – like the denigration of others – is bound up with securing the resources groups of individuals need in order to survive. This imperative operates at international, national, regional and local levels. Even at home we can react very differently to people when they move from the pavement outside our house to approach our front door as we assess in various ways the level of threat they might pose to us.

Religion often provides a group within a nation – or a nation itself – with the cultural justification to lay claim to certain territorial resources and to defend them against all others as a God-given right. There are few stronger combinations for national survival and the pursuit of power than the claim that a particular piece of land not only belongs to, but has also been promised to, a particular nation by God. Especially if it is a fertile area that is bordered by inhospitable desert.

Jesus, however, taught that the kingdom of God was vastly different from the territorial kingdom of Israel. As we have already seen, he spoke of a kingdom that lay within people's hearts (Luke 17.21). Its boundaries are formed or broken by the quality of authentic love we show or fail to show in our lives. His politics were to do with peace rather than worldly power.

He believed not in the survival of the fittest but in the processes of creative love where the marginalized, the weak, the lost and the unloved are cherished and valued as highly as everyone else. He showed that it is more creative to share – rather than fight over – the resources of the world. I am defined not by what I possess but by who I am. And who I am largely depends on what I am prepared to give away. And the most precious gift I have to give is the creative love of God in and through myself.

So rather than ring-fencing our resources, Christ calls the strong to share them in support of the weak and unproductive. In Jesus' teaching in what is called the Sermon on the Mount (Matt. 5—7) he outlines the priorities of the kingdom. Here we can see most clearly how the cyclical loops of negative survival behaviour can be severed.

Jesus spoke not only about the need for us to love our enemies but also about our need to give of our excess to those in need in a way that does not demean them. Charity given out of selfish interests does not promote Divinity in others. 'I am' – by definition – a servant of others. It is not my intention to manipulate others to preserve who I am, for only God can do that.

In loving others, I am not expected to charge interest or even expect a return. This is what it means to love others as I am loved. I ask them who they are and they enable me to be who I am. As I am, so they are too. We discover Divinity within ourselves yet deny it every time we keep it to ourselves. Life is not for holding on to but for giving away. In giving we receive (Luke 6.38). In dying we live (2 Cor. 6.9). By surrendering the world, we gain our eternal selves (Mark 8.36).

Tragically, those who were caught up in the rites and rules of established politics and religion at the time of Jesus rejected the emergence of creative love in the life of the Son of God. Maybe with the best possible motives, they felt that security was to be found in national identity and territorial rites.

Jesus wept over Jerusalem not simply because he knew its people would ignore his message and kill him but because he knew what far-reaching consequences this refusal would cause for creation. He was the way by which we are supposed to discover the reason and the means to live in peace with those of other nationalities and faith communities. Tragically, Jesus is largely ignored, and with devastating long-term results not only for the Middle East but also for the world.

This conflict between the love of the universal Christ and those who prefer to live by power has continued throughout history. The twentieth century in particular witnessed horrific episodes of ethnic conflict and ethnic cleansing. There are now countless crosses on countless hills throughout the world. Countless ways in which we and millions of others might say, 'I am not the person God has called me to be.'

This leaves me feeling ashamed. In the West today people are encouraged to define who they are by what they do and what they possess. There is so little time and space to discover who I am. Christians are the custodians of the way to the formation of a new humanity of which Jesus is the template. Yet in the West you wouldn't believe it by the way we Christians live. We live as materialists, like everyone else.

It is even more important, therefore, if we are to find the peace of God that surpasses all understanding (Phil. 4.7), that we learn how our prayers can descend from our heads into our hearts. The word used in the New Testament for repentance is *metanoia*, meaning a renewal or change of mind. In this sense, all prayer is repentant prayer.

One of the oldest such prayers in the history of the Church is the Jesus Prayer, 'Lord Jesus Christ, Son of God, have mercy on me, a sinner.' While grounded in repentance, this prayer is about so much more, and by constant and devoted use it moves from the cerebral to the cardiac – from the head to the heart – setting the believer free to be with God and to be still in his presence. This is like – though not the same as – the prayer of contemplative presence where we find the heart of ourselves 'simply in touch with him'.

At one time I would have interpreted the will of God in terms of his plans and strategies for the security of myself and others, and my praying was about trying to preserve this at all costs. But if I now contemplate the will of God it appears no longer to be about the politics of self-preservation but about the power of his love. And this cannot but lead me to a place of deep and prayerful peace: 'You should wish for your affairs to turn out, not as you think best, but according to God's will. Then you will be undisturbed and thankful in prayer.'[17]

Although I can feel intimidated by all of this, I also feel energized and empowered. At long last I can see a new purpose in being a member of the church community today. I've moved away from the model of traditional theism, with God seriously grand up there and me simply grovelling down here.

I'm no longer screaming at him to reach into the world from the comfort of his celestial recliner to intervene in the affairs of his creation. I have got away from the guilt that destroys lives. I realize God doesn't need me to beg behind a sacrifice in order to get his attention. I no longer see the perfection of Christ as something that separates me from him in my experience of life. And when tragedy strikes, God is more peacefully present in my praying than ever, 'by whom, and with whom, and in whom, in the unity of the Holy Spirit, all honour and glory be yours, almighty Father, for ever and ever'.[18]

Moreover, I can relate with greater honesty to the Holy Spirit within creation as the emergence of love through the history of the universe. I have found him as the basis of all human being and becoming. What more can I want? Nothing. What more can I do? Everything!

I can begin by avoiding from now on the gospel message that appears to offer justification for our tribal loyalties and inter-tribal rivalry.

I can challenge our insecurity when it promotes judgemental attitudes about others.

Wherever I go, I can define my discipleship in opposition to the evil of the evolutionary drives that slow and sometimes stifle the work of the Spirit.

I can cease to speak of church community – *koinonia* – as Sunday congregations and synods and talk more in terms of those bound together by healing love.

I can cease to invite others to join the church membership in terms of asking them to sign up to a credal formula. Instead, I can invite them to experience the incarnation, the 'I am' in them.

I can promote a church life characterized predominantly by radical love rather than rites of passage. My traditional discipleship has been convicted and found guilty for the way it makes me feel outwardly respectable while leaving me unchanged within.

I realize now that for years I have been acting out a role. I have not been who I am. Jesus defines hypocrites such as myself by using some words of Isaiah:

> This people honours me with their lips,
> but their hearts are far from me;
> in vain do they worship me,
> teaching human precepts as doctrines
> (Mark 7.6–7)

But no more.

I prayed that I should know how to die and I died. I now know not only how to die but also how to live.

More importantly, alive or dead, I am prayerfully now who I am.

Resurrection.

A prayer for the love of Christ

Creator God,
source of the universe
and Spirit of life
may I learn to see you
in all things
that as my heart
rises above
my fallen desires
my prayers
will lead me
to
the love of
your Son
Jesus Christ.

Notes

Introduction

1 Michael S. Gazzaniga, *The Ethical Brain* (Dana Press, 2005), p. 172.
2 Matthew 27.45b: one of the 'words' of Jesus from the cross, 'My God, my God, why have you forsaken me?'
3 See John Shelby Spong, *A New Christianity for a New World* (HarperSanFrancisco, 2001), p. 192.

1: Crying out of love

1 'Though wise men at their end know dark is right/Because their words had forked no lightning they/Do not go gentle into that good night.' Dylan Thomas, 'Do not go gentle . . .', *New Oxford Book of English Verse*, ed. Helen Gardner (Oxford University Press, 1972), p. 942.
2 John Polkinghorne, *Quarks, Chaos and Christianity* (Triangle/SPCK, 1997), p. 53.
3 Denis Edwards, *The God of Evolution* (Paulist Press, 1999), p. 72.
4 Thomas à Kempis, *The Imitation of Christ*, Book 2.11 (Penguin Books, first published 1952), p. 88.
5 The scapegoat was a goat used as part of the sacrificial ceremonies on the Day of Atonement in Judaism when there was a Temple in Jerusalem. This practice is described in Leviticus 16 where the High Priest is described as laying his hands on the head of the goat while he confessed the sins of Israel. The goat was then led away into the wilderness, bearing the sins of the people with it. In Christian theology, this story is often interpreted as prefiguring the self-sacrificial death of Jesus, the lamb of God who takes away the sins of the world.
6 Jeremy Young, *The Cost of Certainty: How Religious Conviction Betrays the Human Psyche* (Darton, Longman & Todd, 2004), p. 100.

7 See Jonathan Schell, *The Fate of the Earth* (Pan Books, 1982), p. 39.
8 Kenneth Greet, *The Big Sin* (Marshall, Morgan & Scott, 1982), p. 15.
9 George Ellis, 'Kenosis as a Unifying Theme for Life and Cosmology' in John Polkinghorne (ed.), *The Work of Love: Creation as Kenosis* (Eerdmans, 2001), p. 120.
10 In the Old Testament Satan has a bet that he can get Job to curse God by visiting a number of unwarranted calamities upon him. God, knowing Job to be 'a blameless and upright man who fears God and turns away from evil', allows the challenge to go ahead. So on one day Job loses his animals – and hence his livelihood – his servants and his sons and daughters. And Job – true to form – reacts by tearing his robe, shaving his head, falling on the ground and worshipping God! He prays, 'Naked I came from my mother's womb, and naked shall I return there; the Lord gave, and the Lord has taken away; blessed be the name of the Lord' (Job 1.21). So here and throughout the book, Job is held up as a faithful man of heroic proportions. But, as I point out, most mortals cannot achieve such an acceptance of disaster when it strikes.
11 *The Cloud of Unknowing*, chs 4 and 34, trans. Clifton Walters (Penguin Books, 1962), pp. 62 and 101.
12 *The Cloud*, ch. 4, p. 63.
13 *The Cloud*, ch. 50, p. 120.
14 *Ruach* is the Hebrew word for spirit, *pneuma* the Greek equivalent. Both mean breath and wind.
15 Alister McGrath, *Dawkins' God: Genes, Memes and the Meaning of Life* (Blackwell, 2005), pp. 157–8.
16 David Martin, *Christian Language in the Secular City* (Ashgate, 2002), p. 177.

2: God, guilt and love

1 'As kingfishers catch fire' from *The Poems of Gerard Manley Hopkins*, ed. W. H. Gardner and N. H. MacKenzie (Oxford University Press, 4th edn, 1970), p. 90.
2 Thomas à Kempis, *The Imitation of Christ*, Book 1.3 (Penguin Books, first published 1952), p. 31.

3 This particular fall–redemption model can be traced back to the Christian theologian St Augustine of Hippo in North Africa (AD 354–430) and was adopted as a central part of the theology of the Church at the Council of Trent (1545–63).

4 Mount Sinai is where God gave the Ten Commandments to Moses (Exod. 20).

5 Thomas Merton, *No Man is an Island* (Burns & Oates, 1955), p. 49.

6 'Most orthodox theologians reject the idea of "original guilt", put forward by Augustine and still accepted (albeit in a mitigated form) by the Roman Catholic Church. The Orthodox Church teaches that humans automatically inherit Adam's corruption and mortality, but not his guilt: they are only guilty in so far as by their own free choice they imitate Adam . . . And Orthodox have never held (as Augustine and many others in the west have done) that unbaptised babies, because tainted with original guilt, are consigned by the just God to the everlasting flames of hell.' See Timothy Ware (Bishop Kallistos of Diokleia), *The Orthodox Church: New Edition* (Penguin Books, 1993), p. 224.

7 Jean-Claude Armen, *Gazelle Boy* (Picador Pan Books, 1976).

8 This picture of God in the face of humanity's experience of suffering predates the one already discussed and associated with Augustine and can be traced back to Irenaeus (AD *c.* 115–190), an early Church Father who studied in Rome before going to Lyons.

9 Refer to John Hick, *Evil and the God of Love* (Macmillan, 1966), p. 255, for a discussion of the image and likeness of God in human beings.

10 Simone Weil, *Gravity and Grace* (Routledge and Kegan Paul, 1963), p. 55.

11 'The sin behind all sin is seen as dualism. Separation. Subject/Object relationships. Fractures and fissures in our relationships. Take any sin: war, burglary, rape, thievery. Every such action involves treating another as an object outside oneself.' Matthew Fox, *Original Blessing* (Bear & Co., 1983), p. 49.

12 See Jeremy Young, *The Cost of Certainty* (Darton, Longman & Todd, 2004), p. 25.

13 Cyprian Smith, *The Way of Paradox: Spiritual Life as Taught by Meister Eckhart* (Darton, Longman & Todd, 1987), p. 64.
14 Elie Wiesel, *Night* (Penguin Books, 1981), p. 77.

3: Falling out of love

1 *The Collected Poems of Theodore Roethke* (Faber & Faber, 1968), p. 37.
2 See, for example, Volker Kuster, *The Many Faces of Jesus Christ* (SCM Press, 1999).
3 Refer to Austin Farrer, *Love Almighty and Ills Unlimited* (Collins, 1962), p. 59.
4 Pseudo-Dionysius, *The Mystical Theology* ch. 5, trans. Colm Luibheid, The Classics of Western Spirituality (Paulist Press, 1987), p. 141.
5 Sheila Cassidy, *Sharing the Darkness* (Darton, Longman & Todd, 1988), pp. 67–76.
6 From 'What can I tell my bones?', *Roethke, Collected Poems*, p. 173.
7 *The Cloud of Unknowing and Other Works* (Penguin Books, 1978), p. 63.
8 Thomas Merton, *New Seeds of Contemplation* (New Directions, 1972), p. 185.
9 I have developed this understanding of the story of Jacob more fully in *Renewing Faith in Ordained Ministry* (SPCK, 2004).
10 See the story of Jacob's dream at Bethel, Genesis 28.10–22.
11 John Hunt, *Bringing God Back Down to Earth* (O Books, 2004), p. 262.
12 See Timothy Ware (Bishop Kallistos of Diokleia), *The Orthodox Church: New Edition* (Penguin Books, 1993), p. 235.
13 This may be a distortion of the saying 'Love sinners but despise their deeds' (St Isaac the Syrian who lived in the seventh century). St Isaac, by contrast, does not suggest that you can somehow separate a person's nature from the life-style they have chosen to live.
14 C. S. Lewis, *A Grief Observed* (Faber & Faber, 1961), p. 33.
15 Origen was a man of the people who believed that the message of the Christian faith had to be accessible to all and not just to an intellectual elite. His aim was pastoral rather than

academic. He believed that the gospel message had to be grounded in people's lives, which at the time were often threatened by persecution from various pagan authorities.

16 Methodius of Olympus repudiated this idea and reaffimed the historicity of the Genesis story, together with Epiphanius, Eustathius of Antioch and others. Yet he also had his supporters among whom were Pamphilus and Eusebius of Caesarea.

17 Very simply, Origen's theory is as follows:

(a) In the beginning, God, out of his pure goodness, created a fixed number of beings (essences) – equal with each other in goodness and status – who were capable of rational thought and whom he could keep under the control of his Providence.

(b) Some of these beings, having been given freedom of choice and themselves being capable of change, remained constant in virtue, but others became tired of being good and having a close relationship with God, and rebelled. The first of these beings to resist was the devil, whom God then rejected.

(c) The errant beings 'fell' (from grace) to various depths depending upon the degree of their rebellion. The least affected became angels or archangels, next were those who became humans and the worst fell with the devil to become demons. The fallen beings on earth are meant to do penance for their sin and win restoration with God through chastisement and discipline.

18 Genesis 1.1—2.4a was written sometime in the sixth or fifth century BC, during the time when many Israelites were held in exile in Babylon. Genesis 2.4a—3.24 may well have been written in the tenth century BC, during the reign of King Solomon.

19 See Donald E. Gowan, *Genesis 1—11: From Eden to Babel* (Eerdmans, 1988), pp. 20ff.

20 *The Philokalia*, vol. 2 trans. and ed. G. E. H. Palmer, Philip Sherrard and Kallistos Ware (Faber & Faber Ltd, first published 1981, this paperback edition first published in 1990), p. 83.

21 While there are similarities between the flood stories of Genesis and those in Babylonian mythology, it is most likely

that the first three chapters of Genesis were in particular an assertion among the religions of the region at the time that God is one and the author of all creation. He does not compete with other gods or demi-gods.

22 Farrer, *Love Almighty*, p. 142.

23 Lt Gen. Roméo Dallaire, *Shake Hands with the Devil: The Failure of Humanity in Rwanda* (Arrow Books, 2004), pp. xviii and 347 in particular. See also M. Scott Peck, *Glimpses of the Devil* (Free Press, 2005).

24 'The universe is between 14 and 16 billion years old. This is known from observational astronomy; principally from examination of light from the most distant observable galaxies. Our universe came into existence in a massive burst of energy popularly known as "The Big Bang". In fact, there could have been no "bang" since sound requires a medium in which to travel; and there was none. Nor was there a flash of light since at that earliest stage light had not yet come into existence nor was there a medium (space and time) in which it could propagate.' Revd Dr Stephen Hunt.

25 Here myth and science combine, yet the myth is not completely dependent upon the exact accuracy of the scientific knowledge of any one generation and whether or not there were one or more Big Bangs. There is still much we have to learn.

26 Malcolm Jeeves, 'The Nature of Persons and the Emergence of Kenotic Behaviour' in John Polkinghorne (ed.), *The Work of Love: Creation as Kenosis* (Eerdmans, 2001), p. 84.

27 Andrew Elphinstone, *Freedom, Suffering and Love* (SCM Press, 1976), p. 127.

28 John Steinbeck, *East of Eden* (Penguin Classics, 2000), p. 415.

29 A time in the history of the evolution of the universe when Christ becomes fulfilled in creation and all things are gathered up into God. This is a term preferred by the French Jesuit theologian Pierre Teilhard de Chardin (1881–1955).

30 Denis Edwards, *The God of Evolution* (Paulist Press, 1999), p. 61.

31 The discussion concerning 'first choice' and 'second choice' intentions or the distinction between antecedent and consequent will has a long tradition in philosophical thought. See Peter

Geach, *Providence and Evil: The Stanton Lectures 1971–2* (Cambridge University Press, 1977).

32 Refer to Rosemary Radford Ruether, *Gaia and God: An Ecofeminist Theology of Earth Healing* (SCM Press, 1993), p. 249.

33 Variously described in different ways by Origen, Pseudo-Dionysius the Areopagite and Maximus the Confessor as the *logoi* of creation.

34 This saying has also been attributed to St Athanasius who lived *c.* 296–373.

35 St Symeon the New Theologian, Hymn 16, 21–40, quoted by Hilarion Alfeyev, *The Mystery of Faith* (SPCK, 2002), p. 194.

36 Anne Sexton, *Holocaust Poetry*, comp. Hilda Schiff (Fount, 1995), p. 191.

37 Alistair Maclean, *Hebridean Altars* (Hodder & Stoughton, 1999; first pub. The Moray Press, 1937).

4: Emerging love

1 William Temple, *Christian Faith and Life* (Mowbray, 1994), p. 34.

2 Simone Weil, *Gravity and Grace* (Routledge and Kegan Paul, 1963), p. 35.

3 Julian of Norwich, *Revelations of Divine Love* (Penguin Books, 1966), p. 77.

4 William Blake, 'A Song of Liberty' in David Perkins (ed.), *English Romantic Writers* (Harcourt Brace, 1967), p. 76.

5 Diarmuid O'Murchu, *Quantum Theology* (Crossroad, 2004), p. 108.

6 See E. O. Wilson, *On Human Nature* (Harvard University Press, 1978), p. 1.

7 Bill Bryson, *A Short History of Nearly Everything* (Black Swan, 2004), p. 460.

8 Denis Edwards, *The God of Evolution* (Paulist Press, 1999), p. 90.

9 'Aubade', *Philip Larkin: Collected Poems*, ed. Anthony Thwaite (Marvell Press, 1988), p. 208.

10 John Polkinghorne, *Quarks, Chaos, and Christianity* (Triangle/SPCK, 1997), p. 55.

11 Polkinghorne, *Quarks*, p. 57.

12 O'Murchu, *Quantum Theology*, p. 48.
13 'At the subatomic level, the classical distinction between matter and energy disappears. At the level of the "absolute minimum" the appearance of physical "stuff" disappears into a voidlike web of relationships, relationships in which the whole universe is finally interconnected and in which the observer also stands as part of the process.' Rosemary Radford Ruether, *Gaia and God: An Ecofeminist Theology of Earth Healing* (SCM Press, 1993), p. 249.
14 Malcolm Jeeves, 'The Nature of Persons and the Emergence of Kenotic Behaviour' in John Polkinghorne (ed.), *The Work of Love: Creation as Kenosis* (Eerdmans, 2001), p. 73.
15 'Men never do evil so completely and cheerfully as when they do it from religious conviction.' Blaise Pascal, *Pensées*, Part XIV, No. 895.
16 Among others, see John C. Avise, *The Genetic Gods: Evolution and Belief in Human Affairs* (Harvard University Press, 1998); John Bowker, *Is God a Virus? Genes, Culture and Religion* (SPCK, 1995); Richard Dawkins, *The Selfish Gene* (Granada Publishing, 1978).
17 There is an interesting discussion of the seemingly pervasive nature of consciousness in evolutionary structures in Alister Hardy's *Darwin and the Spirit of Man* (Collins, 1984).
18 See Wilson, *On Human Nature*, pp. 117–19.
19 Paul MacLean, 'The triune brain, emotion and scientific bias' in F. O. Schmidt (ed.), *Neurosciences: Second Study Program* (Rockefeller University Press, 1970), pp. 336–49.
20 Michael S. Gazzaniga, *The Ethical Brain* (Dana Press, 2005), p. 172.
21 Bowker, *Is God a Virus?*, p. 169.
22 Julian of Norwich, *Revelations*, p. 96.

5: Love in person

1 Alexander Schmemann, *For the Life of the World* (St Vladimir's Press, 1995), p. 99.
2 The raising of Jairus' daughter (Luke 8.40–56), the healing of the widow of Nain's son (Luke 7.11–17) and the raising of Lazarus (John 11.1–44).

3 In November 2002 the General Synod of the Church of England, with a two-thirds majority in all three houses, agreed to rescind the Convocation resolutions which exhorted clergy not to permit the remarriage of divorced persons in church.
4 John Bowker, *The Sacred Neuron* (I. B. Tauris, 2005), p. 156.
5 Michael S. Gazzaniga, *The Ethical Brain* (Dana Press, 2005), pp. 153ff.
6 John Main, *Moment of Christ* (Darton, Longman & Todd, 1984), p. 54.
7 This has been attributed to both Clement of Rome and to Irenaeus.
8 Gerd Theissen, *Biblical Faith: An Evolutionary Approach* (SCM Press, 1984), pp. 106ff.
9 This is his favourite title for himself in Mark's Gospel.
10 A traditional Jewish picture taken on by the Church to represent the gathering together of the people of God at the end of time; see Luke 14.15–21.
11 I have used this image of the messianic Banquet in more detail in *Renewing Faith in Ordained Ministry* (SPCK, 2004), pp. 94–9.
12 Alexander Schmemann, *For the Life of the World* (St Vladimir's Press, 1995), p. 113.
13 See a recent study of this by James Cowan, *Francis: A Saint's Way* (Hodder & Stoughton, 2001).
14 Galatians 5.22–26, for example.
15 John Bowker, *Is God a Virus? Genes, Culture and Religion* (SPCK, 1995) p. 135.
16 Olivier Clément, *The Roots of Christian Mysticism* (New City, 1993), p. 96.
17 Evagrios the Solitary (AD 345–99), no. 89, *The Philokalia*, Vol. 1, trans. and ed. G. E. H. Palmer, Philip Sherrard and Kallistos Ware (Faber and Faber Ltd, first published in 1979, first published in Faber paperbacks 1983), p. 66.
18 Eucharistic Prayer F, *Common Worship*, © The Archbishops' Council of the Church of England, 2000.